Company

Now *in* *this* *age* *of* *confusion*
I *have* *need* *for* *your* *company.*

—RICHARD FARIÑA

COMPANY

* A MUSICAL COMEDY *

★

BOOK BY

George Furth

MUSIC AND LYRICS BY

Stephen Sondheim

Originally produced and directed on Broadway

by Harold Prince

RANDOM HOUSE · NEW YORK

For Lee Strasberg and
G. L. Harrington, M.D.

THE SCENE

New York City
NOW

COMPANY *was first presented on April 26, 1970, by Harold Prince, in association with Ruth Mitchell, at the Alvin Theatre in New York City with the following cast:*

ROBERT	Dean Jones
SARAH	Barbara Barrie
HARRY	Charles Kimbrough
SUSAN	Alice Cannon
PETER	John Cunningham
JENNY	Teri Ralston
DAVID	George Coe
AMY	Beth Howland
PAUL	Steve Elmore
JOANNE	Elaine Stritch
LARRY	Charles Braswell
MARTA	Pamela Myers
KATHY	Donna McKechnie
APRIL	Susan Browning

There is no singing or dancing ensemble. Only the members of the cast become the choir, waiters, patrons, etc.

Music and lyrics by Stephen Sondheim
Book by George Furth
Sets and projections designed by Boris Aronson
Costumes by D. D. Ryan
Lighting by Robert Ornbo
Musical direction by Harold Hastings
Orchestrations by Jonathan Tunick
Dance music arrangements by Wally Harper
Musical numbers staged by Michael Bennett
Production directed by Harold Prince

Musical Numbers

ACT ONE

"Company"	Robert and Company
"The Little Things You Do Together"	Joanne and Company
"Sorry-Grateful"	Harry, David and Larry
"You Could Drive a Person Crazy"	Kathy, April and Marta
"Have I Got a Girl for You?"	Larry, Peter, Paul, David and Harry
"Someone Is Waiting"	Robert
"Another Hundred People"	Marta
"Getting Married Today"	Amy, Paul, Jenny and Company

ACT TWO

"Side by Side by Side"	Robert and the Couples
"What Would We Do Without You?"	Robert and the Couples
"Poor Baby"	Sarah, Jenny, Susan, Amy and Joanne
Love Dance	Kathy
"Barcelona"	Robert, April
"The Ladies Who Lunch"	Joanne
"Being Alive"	Robert

Act One

SCENE ONE

The curtain rises on a multi-leveled steel structure indicating various high-rise Manhattan apartments. Two elevators and stairs link the different levels. There are five empty living areas on the various levels of the raised structure. Each of the areas is to denote the apartment of one couple, and it is that same area to which the couple will always return at various points during the action. When cleared, the stage level belongs to ROBERT. For reasons of vision and space, most of the longer scenes are played in this stage-level area, with sections containing furniture moved on. As the scenes change, rear and frontal projections are used to indicate different skylines and city sights.

As the lights come up slowly, ROBERT's apartment slides in on stage level. The five couples are sitting at or standing around a dining-room table. Each of the wives is carrying a gaily wrapped gift box. JOANNE goes to the center of the room and places her present on a coffee table. She is followed by SUSAN, who puts her gift down and smiles at JOANNE, who tokenly smiles back and moves away. JOANNE puts a cigarette in her mouth. LARRY crosses to her, lights his lighter and holds it up. JOANNE chooses to ignore it, lighting her own cigarette. She moves around Larry and returns to the dining-room table.

We hear footsteps in the distance growing louder, and the sound of a key in the lock. At this point the couples scramble for positions around the table and the lights are turned out.

ALL Shhhh!

> (*The door opens and* ROBERT *enters. A glaring spot-
> light hits his face. He jumps*)

ROBERT (*Shielding his face*) What's this? What the hell
is going on around here? Huh? Who is it? Who is that?

ALL (*Intoning*) Surprise.

ROBERT My birthday. It's my birthday. Do you know you
had me scared to death. I was just about to run out of this
place like nobody's business. *I was.* I mean, I didn't know
—I mean, what kind of friends would surprise you on
your thirty-fifth birthday? (*He pauses*) Mine. Then
again, how many times do you get to be thirty-five?
Eleven? (*He pauses*) Okay, come on. Say it and get it
over with. It's embarrassing. Quick. I can't stand it.

ALL (*Intoning*) Happy birthday, Robert.

ROBERT I stood it. Thank you for including me in your
thoughts, your lives, your families. Yes, thank you for
remembering. Thank you.

ALL (*Intoning*) You don't look it.

ROBERT (*Laughs*) Well, I feel it.

ALL (*Intoning*) It's the birthday boy!

ROBERT Now, you've rehearsed. Very good. I am touched.

SUSAN (*Breaking intonation. Excitedly*) I love it when
people are really surprised.

PETER She loves it when people are really surprised.

4

SARAH (*Handing him her gift*) If you don't like it, you can take it back.

ROBERT Well, I haven't even seen it yet.

SARAH I mean, though, if you don't like it—

HARRY Why don't you wait until the man looks at the thing?

ROBERT I know I'll like it.

SARAH Why don't you just take it back?

HARRY For God's sake, he just said he likes it.

SARAH Pretend not to notice Harry, Robert. I think I'll leave.

(*She starts to move away*)

HARRY I was being funny, Sarah. We could stay a little longer.

(*They both come eye to eye, and slowly, very slowly, sink stiffly, simultaneously, into two chairs as the action continues*)

PETER (*Throwing his present to* ROBERT) Hey, Bobby, take ours back too.

AMY (*Bringing hers to* ROBERT) Here's from Paul and me. If I were you, I would take it back and get the money. It cost so much I fainted.

PAUL It did not, Robert. It's a sweater.

AMY You told him what it was! (*To* ROBERT) Well, when I saw the price tag, I thought it was a house.

JOANNE (*As* JENNY *starts toward* ROBERT) Miss, Miss. YOU! Yes, you! Tell him to take yours back and get the money. It's not the gift, it's the cost that counts.

JENNY (*Handing her present to* ROBERT) Who *is* that?

JOANNE That is I, Miss. I am very rich and I am married to him (*Indicates her husband*) and I'd introduce him, but I forgot his name.

ROBERT (*Quickly*) Haven't you two met?

JOANNE Pass, baby. Pass. There's no one here I want to meet. Except her. She's crazy. (*Points to* AMY) And him. He's a looker. (*Points to* PETER, *going over to him*) The rest are Lois and Larry Loser—(*She takes* PETER's *drink from him*) Here's to you, winner.
(*She downs the drink*)

PETER (*Smiling, flattered, to* JOANNE) I find you quite fascinating. Quite delightful. Quite—

JOANNE You just blew it.
(*She puts the empty glass back in* PETER's *hand and moves away from him*)

LARRY Many happy returns of the day, old man.

JENNY (*Breaking the tension. Gaily*) David is now going to deliver *our* greeting. Go on, sweetheart.

DAVID (*Looks at her, stunned. A moment; then*) Robert, happy birthday from us.
(*An awkward salute and smile to* ROBERT)

PETER (*Giving him that friendly punch on the arm*) And may this year bring you fame, fortune, and your first wife.

6

ALL   Hear, hear!

ROBERT   Listen, I'm fine without the three.

JOANNE   You bet your ass, baby.

(AMY *slips out*)

SUSAN (*To* JOANNE)   He might have meant that super-ciliously.

JOANNE (*A "what-do-you-know" look to* SUSAN)   Oooo, isn't she darling with all that free help.

SUSAN (*In a whimpering tone*)   I meant he could have been being funny, is all I meant.

(*She sits down*)

JOANNE (*Sitting down, across from* SUSAN)   Now, don't cry. Don't cry or I'll push your chair over.

LARRY (*Crosses behind* JOANNE's *chair*)   She's kidding ya. She's a great kidder.

ROBERT (*Nervously*)   All right. Let's cut out the many happy returns, and that is about enough about me. I am just indeed lucky to have all of you. I mean, when you've got friends like mine . . .

AMY (*Enters, with a lighted cake*)   Well, our blessings, Robert.

(JENNY *starts the group singing "Happy Birthday," which comes out in monotone*)

AMY (*Interrupting the song*)   Blow out your candles and get your wish.

JENNY   Don't tell your wish, Bobby, or it won't come true.

SUSAN   You have to close your eyes and blow them all out.

JOANNE   SHUT—UP!

LARRY   (*Laughing*) That's just her way of fooling. (JOANNE *laughs*) See what I mean?

PETER   Talk about your sense of humor! Terrific!

AMY   Be sure you make it a good one, Robert.

> (*He closes his eyes, wishes and blows, but only half the candles go out. The wives hurriedly blow out the rest. As the following lines are spoken, each couple picks up a piece of* ROBERT's *furniture and carries it out*)

JENNY   You still get your wish. He still gets his wish!

SUSAN   He does? It must be a new rule!

AMY   Sure you do.

JOANNE   (*Moving away*) Don't believe a word of it.

> (*Music begins under, sounding like a busy signal*)

SARAH   Of course you do.

ROBERT   Oh, I know it. I will. Actually, I didn't wish for anything.

LARRY   He's kidding. You gotta be kidding.

DAVID   Anyway, don't tell it.

PETER   Tell it if it's dirty.

PAUL   They say you're not supposed to tell it.

AMY Paul's right. Don't tell.

HARRY Anyway, Robert, you're in your prime—thirty-five.

SARAH Harry, hush! You don't tell a person's age at our ages.

> (*Now* ROBERT *stands alone in a completely denuded room, his friends now watching from their living areas above. He faces front, listening*)

JENNY (*Sings*)
    Bobby . . .
PETER
    Bobby . . .
AMY
    Bobby baby . . .
PAUL
    Bobby bubi . . .
JOANNE
    Robby . . .
SUSAN
    Robert darling . . .
DAVID
    Bobby, we've been trying to call you.
JENNY
    Bobby . . .
LARRY
    Bobby . . .
AMY
    Bobby baby . . .
PAUL
    Bobby bubi . . .

SARAH
    Angel, I've got something to tell you.

HARRY
  Bob . . .
LARRY
  Rob-o . . .
JOANNE
  Bobby love . . .
SUSAN
  Bobby honey . . .

AMY and PAUL
  Bobby, we've been trying to reach you all day.

LARRY
  Bobby . . .
HARRY
  Bobby . . .
PETER
  Bobby baby . . .
SARAH
  Angel . . .
JOANNE
  Darling . . .

DAVID and JENNY
  The kids were asking, Bobby . . .

HARRY
  Bobby . . .
SUSAN
  Robert . . .
JOANNE
  Robby . . .
PETER
  Bob-o . . .
LARRY and JOANNE
  Bobby, there was something we wanted to say.

SARAH and HARRY
Bobby . . .

PAUL
Bobby bubi . . .

AMY
Sweetheart . . .

SUSAN
Sugar . . .

DAVID and JENNY
Your line was busy.

PETER
What have you been up to, kiddo?

AMY and PAUL
Bobby, Bobby, how have you been?

HARRY
Fella . . .

SARAH
Sweetie . . .

HARRY and SARAH
How have you been?

PETER and SUSAN
Bobby, Bobby, how have you been?

DAVID, JENNY, JOANNE and LARRY
Stop by on your way home—

AMY and PAUL
Seems like weeks since we talked to you!

HARRY and SARAH
Bobby, we've been thinking of you!

PETER and SUSAN
Bobby, we've been thinking of you!

DAVID, JENNY, JOANNE and LARRY
Drop by anytime.

AMY and PAUL
> Bobby, there's a concert on Tuesday.

DAVID and JENNY
> Hank and Mary get into town tomorrow.

PETER and SUSAN
> How about some scrabble on Sunday?

SARAH and HARRY
> Why don't we all go to the beach?

JOANNE and LARRY
> Bob, we're having people in Saturday night.

HARRY and SARAH
> Next weekend?

JENNY
> Bobby . . .

PETER
> Bobby . . .

AMY
> Bobby, baby . . .

DAVID and JENNY
> Whatcha doing Thursday?

HARRY
> Bobby . . .

SARAH
> Angel . . .

PAUL
> Bobby bubi . . .

SARAH and HARRY
> Time we got together, is Wednesday all right?

AMY
> Bobby . . .

LARRY
> Rob-o . . .

SUSAN
> Bobby honey . . .

AMY and PAUL
> Eight o'clock on Monday.

JOANNE
> Robby darling . . .

PETER
> Bobby fella . . .

PETER and JOANNE
> Bobby baby . . .

ALL
> Bobby, come on over for dinner!
> We'll be so glad to see you!
> Bobby, come on over for dinner!
> Just be the three of us,
> Only the three of us,
> We loooooove you!

ROBERT
> Phone rings, door chimes, in comes company!
> No strings, good times, room hums, company!
> Late nights, quick bites, party games,
> Deep talks, long walks, telephone calls,
> Thoughts shared, souls bared, private names,
> All those photos up on the walls
> "With love,"
> With love filling the days,
> With love seventy ways,
> "To Bobby, with love"
> From all
> Those
> Good and crazy people, my friends,
> Those

Good and crazy people, my married friends!
And that's what it's all about, isn't it?
That's what it's really about,
Really about!

(*The three girlfriends,* APRIL, KATHY *and* MARTA
enter)

APRIL
Bobby . . .
KATHY
Bobby . . .
MARTA
Bobby baby . . .
PAUL
Bobby bubi . . .
JOANNE
Robby . . .
SUSAN
Robert darling . . .
SARAH
Angel, will you do me a favor?
LARRY
Bobby . . .
AMY
Bobby . . .

ROBERT
Name it, Sarah.
JENNY
Bobby baby . . .
PAUL
Bobby bubi . . .

PETER
Listen, pal, I'd like your opinion . . .

HARRY
    Bob . . .
LARRY
    Rob-o . . .

ROBERT
    Try me, Peter.
KATHY
    Bobby love . . .
MARTA
    Bobby honey . . .

LARRY and AMY
    Bobby, there's a problem—I need your advice . . .
APRIL and PAUL
    Bobby . . .
MARTA and HARRY
    Bobby . . .
KATHY and PETER
    Bobby baby . . .
SARAH
    Angel . . .
JOANNE
    Darling . .

APRIL, MARTA and KATHY
    Just half an hour . . .
ROBERT
    Amy, can I call you back tomorrow?
DAVID and JENNY
    Honey, if you'd visit the kids once or twice . . .
SARAH and PETER
    Bobby . . .
JOANNE and HARRY
    Bobby . . .

PAUL and MARTA
> Bobby bubi . . .

AMY
> Sweetheart . . .

SUSAN
> Sugar . . .

APRIL, MARTA and KATHY
> What's happened to you?

ROBERT
> Jenny, I could take them to the zoo on Friday.

WIVES
> Bobby . . . Bobby, where have you been?

HUSBANDS
> Fella . . . kiddo, where have you been?

GIRLS
> Bobby . . . Bobby, how have you been?

HARRY, SARAH, PETER and SUSAN
> Stop by on your way home . . .

ROBERT
> Susan, love, I'll make it after seven if I can.

WIVES
> Bobby, dear, I don't mean to pry.

HUSBANDS
> Bobby, we've been thinking of you!

GIRLS
> Bobby, we've been thinking of you!

PAUL, AMY, JOANNE, LARRY, DAVID and JENNY
> Drop by anytime . . .

ROBERT
> Sorry, Paul, I made a date with Larry and Joanne.

WIVES
> Bobby, dear, it's none of my business . . .

HUSBANDS

Lookit, pal, I have to work Thursday evening . . .

WIVES

Darling, you've been looking peculiar . . .

HUSBANDS

Bobby boy, you know how I hate the opera . . .

WIVES

Funny thing, your name came up only last night.

ROBERT

Harry . . . David . . . Kathy, I . . .

GIRLS

I shouldn't say this but . . .

ROBERT

April . . . Marta . . . Listen, people . . .

WIVES

Bobby, we've been worried, you sure you're all right?

HUSBANDS

Bobby . . . Bobby . . . Bobby baby . . .

GIRLS

Did I do something wrong?

HUSBANDS

Bobby bubi, Bobby fella, Bobby, Bobby,

ALL

Bobby, come on over for dinner!
We'll be so glad to see you!
Bobby, come on over for dinner!
Just be the three of us,
Only the three of us,
We LOOOOOOOOOOOOOOVE you!

Phone rings, door chimes, in comes company!
No strings, good times, just chums, company!

Late nights, quick bites, party games,
Deep talks, long walks, telephone calls,
Thoughts shared, souls bared, private names,
All those photos up on the walls
"With love,"
With love filling the days,
With love seventy ways,
"To Bobby, with love"
From all
Those
Good and crazy people, my friends,
Those good and crazy people, my married friends!
And that's what it's all about, isn't it?
That's what it's really about, isn't it?
That's what it's really about, really about!

HUSBANDS

Isn't it? Isn't it? Isn't it? Isn't it?

WIVES and **GIRLS**

LOOOOOOVE

HUSBANDS

Isn't it? Isn't it? Isn't it? Isn't it?

ROBERT

You I love and you I love and you and you I love
And you I love and you I love and you and you I love,
I love you!

ALL

Company! Company! Company, lots of company!
Years of company! Love is company!
Company!

(*The ringing of telephones and doorbells and city
sounds are heard. The following lines are spoken
simultaneously as the company moves and exits in
the frantic pace of New York streets and lives*)

JOANNE   What time was that?

LARRY   Five o'clock, I think, Joanne.

JOANNE   Thank God, cocktail hour!

APRIL   Final departure call for NSEW Airlines Flight One-nineteen. Will the passengers that have not boarded please do so.

SARAH   Harry, it's the door. I'll get it.

HARRY   I've got it.

SARAH   *I'll* get it. I always do.

PETER   What the hell is that noise?

SUSAN   They're cleaning the building next door, or tearing it down.

KATHY   Taxi! Taxi! Oh, please, please!

MARTA   Will you stop blowing that horn, you dodo!

AMY   Paul, what is that noise?

PAUL   I don't hear anything.

JENNY   Oh, David, the phone!

DAVID   I'll get it.

JENNY   Oh, the kids. It's gonna wake up the kids.

(*They have all exited*)

SCENE TWO

The scene is SARAH *and* HARRY's *living room on the ground floor of a garden apartment. Chic. Classy. There is much laughing, giggling, smiling and* affection.

ROBERT *is their dinner guest. He tries to maintain this atmosphere of conviviality, even when he's not sure of what is happening. The three have finished a long dinner and are seated, having coffee in the living room.*

SARAH (*Pouring coffee*) There's cinnamon in the coffee, Robert . . . The odd taste is cinnamon. Sugar and cream?

ROBERT Both. May I have lots of both?

SARAH Of course you may.

HARRY Do you want some brandy in it, Robert? Or do you just want some brandy?

ROBERT You having some?

SARAH We don't drink, but you have some, you darling. Go ahead.

HARRY Or do you want a real drink? We have anything you want.

ROBERT Well, Harry, if you don't mind, could I have some bourbon?

HARRY Right.

*(He goes to the bar and begins the elaborate prepa-
ration of* ROBERT'S *drink)*

SARAH Sweetheart!

HARRY Okay, darling.

ROBERT *(As* HARRY *gets the bourbon)* Are you both on
the wagon? Sarah? You're not on the wagon?

SARAH Goodness, Robert, all the questions! Or do you
just collect trivia like some old quiz kid? We spend half
of our lives with you and now you notice Harry's on the
wagon?

HARRY A year and a half.

SARAH No, love. Just a year.

HARRY It was a year in February. It's a year and a half
now.

SARAH I know for a fact next month it will be a year.

HARRY And a half.

SARAH One year. Count it, one! Harry got arrested for
being drunk, and quit out of some kind of humiliation.

HARRY I quit to see if I could is actually what happened.
C'mon, I must have told you about all that.

ROBERT Never. You never mentioned it or I never would
have brought you the bourbon. How were you arrested?

SARAH Another question! Here, why don't you have one
of these brownies you brought?

HARRY   I was in California on business and I really got soused one night and these guys drove me back to my hotel, but instead of going in, I walked down to the corner to get something to eat to sober up.

(*He has poured the bourbon into* ROBERT's *glass, and sniffs it longingly*)

SARAH (*Interrupting*)   You said it was three blocks away.

HARRY   No, just the corner.

SARAH (*In a stage whisper to* ROBERT)   Three blocks away.

HARRY   Anyway, this patrol car stopped me and said, "You're drunk." I said, "Drunk? I'm clobbered." He said, "I'm taking you in." "Take me to my hotel, for God's sake," I said. "It's just on the corner."

(*He cracks the ice and adds the soda*)

SARAH   Three blocks away.

(ROBERT *moves to the bar and reaches for his drink, but is stopped by* HARRY, *who indicates that the lemon peel has not yet been added*)

HARRY   Anyway, they mugged me and booked me for being drunk. Unbelievable. California is a police state, though. And then, Robert, the very next time I was out there, I got arrested all over again—drunk driving. I only had wine—

SARAH   Only five bottles . . .

HARRY   And I *insisted* on taking a drunk test. I flunked it by one point.

(*He adds lemon peel to the drink with a flourish*)

SARAH   And that is when you quit, precious. He always thinks it was the first arrest, but it was the second. We never told you that? Curious, I thought Harry had told *everybody.*

HARRY   (*His gaze fixed on* ROBERT's *drink*)   Anyway, I quit to see if I really had a drinking problem, and I don't.

SARAH   Just a problem drinking.

(ROBERT *finally takes the drink from* HARRY, *breaking* HARRY's "trance")

ROBERT   Do you miss it?

SARAH   See how you talk in questions! Harry, do you miss it?

HARRY   No. No, I really don't.

SARAH (*Loud whisper to* ROBERT)   Yes. Yes, he really does. (*Full voice, and a wave to* HARRY) Hi, darling.

HARRY   Anyway, I stopped. Haven't had a drink since.

SARAH   Whoops.

HARRY   What's whoops? I haven't had a drink since.

SARAH (*She sings this*)   At Evelyn and George's wedding.

HARRY   A toast, for God's sake. Sorry, Robert, you must have noticed how staggering falling-down drunk I got on one swallow of champagne.

SARAH   I *never* said you got drunk, but you did have the champagne.

HARRY   A swallow. One swallow.

SARAH   And it was gone. An elephant's swallow.

ROBERT   I'd like to ask for another bourbon, but I'm terrified.

(HARRY *grabs the glass and runs back to the bar*)

SARAH   Darling Robert, put a nipple on the bottle for all we care. Don't you want a brownie?

ROBERT   God, no. I'll bust.

SARAH   Bust? *You* bust! You skinny thing. Just look at you. Bones. You're skin and bones. I bet when you get on a scale it goes the other way—minus.

ROBERT   Well, thank you, Sarah. I am touched and honored. And I think I was just insulted.

SARAH   (*Takes a brownie from the box*) Oh, Robert, I was praying that you'd eat just one so I could watch.

ROBERT   Sarah! Is it possible you've become a food voyeur?

SARAH   Mexican food. What I crave without cease is Mexican food. With all the Tabasco sauce in the world.

HARRY   (*With his back to* SARAH, *but knowing what she's up to*) Don't eat that brownie!

SARAH   I'm not. I'm just smelling it. Oh, Robert, you eat one!

ROBERT Not with bourbon. (*Takes his second drink*)
Thank you, Harry.

> (HARRY *looks upset, as he hasn't the lemon nor his other "extras"*)

SARAH And chocolate. I'd kill for chocolate. Or a baked
potato with sour cream and chives. Doesn't that just make
you writhe? Or hot sourdough bread and all the butter
there is.

HARRY Chili.

SARAH Oh, chili, dear God, yes, chili!

HARRY Manicotti.

SARAH Manicotti. One teaspoon of manicotti.

HARRY Sara Lee cake.

SARAH Sara Lee cake! Sara Lee is the most phenomenal
woman since Mary Baker Eddy.

HARRY How about sweet and sour shrimp?

SARAH How about sweet and sour pork?

> (*She pretends to pass out by falling behind the sofa, but* ROBERT *has seen her stick a brownie in her mouth on the way down. She eats it, hidden from their sight behind the sofa.* ROBERT *watches this, and turns in time to see* HARRY *stealing one swallow of bourbon*)

ROBERT (*Crosses to the sofa and calls to the hidden* SARAH)
I get the impression you guys are on diets.

HARRY Not me. Sarah.

SARAH (*Rises and crosses from behind the sofa, still chewing*) Look at these pants. You can put your fist in there. That's how much weight I've lost.

HARRY She always does that. Look, I can put my fist in my pants too, you know. She thinks I buy that.

SARAH Darling, I've lost eight pounds already.

HARRY It's the magazines, Robert. Did you ever look at any of those women's magazines? Pages and pages of cakes and pies and roasts and potatoes. I bet Sarah subscribes to about forty magazines. It's a sickness. We're up to our ass in magazines.

SARAH I read them all.

HARRY Don't.

SARAH Do.

HARRY Look at this, Robert. Wrestling. She even subscribes to a magazine on wrestling.

SARAH Karate, not wrestling. It's karate.

HARRY Wouldn't you like to see it? All those fat broads in her gym learning karate. What wouldn't you give to see that?

SARAH Strangely enough, darling, I'm terribly good at it.

ROBERT How long have you been studying it?

SARAH (*To* ROBERT, *in a mock-scolding tone*) Who asked that question? Oh, Robert! Seven months.

HARRY Show us some karate.

SARAH   No. Robert, would you like some more coffee, love?
You, Harry?

HARRY   No. I want some karate. I want to see how my
money is being wasted.

SARAH   No.

ROBERT   Do one thing.

SARAH   No.

ROBERT (*Flirtatiously*) Come on, Sarah, I really would
give anything to see you do just one. I bet you are *excellent*. Hey, I'll be your partner.

SARAH (*Responding girlishly*) No. Oh, Harry, this is embarrassing.

HARRY   Aw, come on.

SARAH   My God—all right.

HARRY   Hooray!

SARAH   One throw!

HARRY   Hooray!

SARAH   Harry, do you want to stand there?

HARRY   Where?

SARAH   There.

HARRY   All right. I'm standing here. Now what?

(SARAH, *with intense concentration, goes into her karate preparation ritual, complete with kneebends, deep-breathing, grunts and a variety of chops and holds*)

SARAH Okay. Now just come at me.

HARRY Okay.

(*He does, and she lets out a piercing samurai sound, "Hyieeeee," flipping him spread-eagle to the floor.* SARAH *does a Japanese bow to* HARRY, *and does a feminine tiptoe dance to the sofa, where she lies majestically and adorably, looking at her fingernails*)

ROBERT Fantastic. That's hysterical.

HARRY (*Gets up and moves away, doing some sort of twist to loosen his back from the impact of the fall*) Actually, I could have prevented that.

SARAH How?

HARRY By blocking it.

SARAH No, that can't be blocked.

HARRY It certainly can. I just didn't do it.

SARAH Anyway, Robert, that can't be blocked.

HARRY Let's do it again.

SARAH All right, darling.

(*She is the sweet killer, arranging herself*)

HARRY   I'll come at you again.

SARAH   Okay. (*He goes at her. She attempts the same thing and he blocks it by lifting her and putting her over his shoulder. Taken by surprise,* SARAH *quickly reworks the movement in her mind and comes up with her mistake*) Oh, I see. Put me down. Okay, do it again.

> (*He does it again and she overcomes his block, throwing him again. She then gives a karate scream and jumps on top of him, pinning him down.* ROBERT, HARRY *and* SARAH *freeze in their positions.* JOANNE *appears and looks for a moment with wry detachment at the pair on the floor. She sings "The Little Things You Do Together"*)

JOANNE
It's the little things you do together,
Do together,
Do together,
That make perfect relationships.
The hobbies you pursue together,
Savings you accrue together,
Looks you misconstrue together
That make marriage a joy.
Mm-hm . . .

> (*They break the freeze*)

ROBERT   (*To break the tension, forcing a laugh*)   That's very good.

HARRY   Once more. Do it once more.

ROBERT   Harry, could I have another bourbon?

(There is a much more serious look on both of their faces now . . . HARRY *lunges at her. They block each other and are caught in a power struggle)*

HARRY   Give up?

SARAH   Do you?

HARRY   I've got you.

SARAH   I've got *you.*

HARRY   Do you want to do it again?

SARAH   All right. You break first.

HARRY   Uh-uh. You break first.

SARAH   We can just stay here.

HARRY   All right with me. Fine with me.

ROBERT   You're both very good.

HARRY   I could get out of this, you know.

SARAH   Try it.

*(*HARRY *kicks a foot behind her two feet, knocking her to the floor. He's on top of her, pinning her down)*

HARRY   Okay, I tried it.

*(*SARAH *grabs* HARRY *by his shirt and somersaults him over her head, so that he ends up flat on his back on the floor. She quickly stands up, grabs* HARRY's *arm and pins him down with her foot, hold-*

ing him in place with an arm pull. Groaning loudly in agony, HARRY *beats on the floor with his free hand*)

SARAH   Uncle?

HARRY   Uncle, your ass!

(HARRY, SARAH *and* ROBERT *freeze*)

JOANNE
It's the little things you share together,
Swear together,
Wear together,
That make perfect relationships.
The concerts you enjoy together,
Neighbors you annoy together,
Children you destroy together,
That keep marriage intact.

It's not so hard to be married
When two maneuver as one,
It's not so hard to be married
And, Jesus Christ, is it fun.

It's sharing little winks together,
Drinks together,
Kinks together,
That makes marriage a joy.

It's bargains that you shop together,
Cigarettes you stop together,
Clothing that you swap together,
That make perfect relationships.

Uh-huh . . .
Mm-hm . . .

(They break the freeze, and SARAH *and* HARRY *prepare for a third fall.* ROBERT *gets up from his chair with his empty glass and tries to cross the room to get a refill)*

ROBERT   Could I have another bourbon?

(Inadvertently he finds himself between SARAH *and* HARRY, *and suddenly he is hit from the front by* HARRY *and from the rear by* SARAH. *All three go down to the floor with much noise. Intertwined, the three freeze. The other married couples enter and sing with* JOANNE)

ALL

It's not talk of God and the decade ahead that
Allow you to get through the worst.
It's "I do" and "You don't" and "Nobody said that"
And "Who brought the subject up first?"
It's the little things, the little things, the little
        things . . .
It's the little things, the little things, the little
        things . . .
The little ways you try together,
Cry together,
Lie together,
That make perfect relationships.
Becoming a cliché together,
Growing old and gray together
JOANNE
Withering away together
ALL
That makes marriage a joy.

MEN
>It's not so hard to be married,

WOMEN
>It's much the simplest of crimes.

MEN
>It's not so hard to be married,

JOANNE
>I've done it three or four times.

JENNY
>It's people that you hate together,

PAUL and AMY
>Bait together,

PETER and SUSAN
>Date together,

ALL
>That make marriage a joy.

DAVID
>It's things like using force together,

LARRY
>Shouting till you're hoarse together,

JOANNE
>Getting a divorce together,

ALL
>That make perfect relationships.

>Uh-huh . . .
>Kiss, kiss . . .
>Mm-hm.

>(JOANNE *and the others leave. Finally* ROBERT,
>SARAH *and* HARRY *break at the same time; all are*
>*panting for air*)

ROBERT   My . . . wow . . . How 'bout that? Huh?

HARRY (*Laughing*)   I had you there . . .

SARAH (*Laughing*)   I had *you* there . . .

(*They start for each other again, but* ROBERT *steps between them*)

ROBERT   I'd say it was a draw. (*They say nothing, trying to pull themselves together*) Wow. Look at the time. I've got to get going.

SARAH and HARRY   Awww!

ROBERT   Wow. Listen, I had a great time.

SARAH (*Still panting hard*)   So did we.

HARRY (*Panting*)   Great to see you. Sure you wouldn't care for a nightcap?

ROBERT   Right! (HARRY *starts for the bar*) I mean, no! I mean, will I see you soon?

SARAH (*With a slight smile*)   Don't answer that, Harry. He gets no more questions, that sneaky Pete.

(*Gives* ROBERT *an affectionate peck on the cheek*)

ROBERT (*Still panting*)   Wow. (*The music of "Bobby Baby" is heard in the orchestra; there is a slight and self-conscious pause*) Thanks again.

(*He leaves the scene slowly, utterly bewildered.* HARRY *heads for the bar. With his fingertip he catches a drop of liquor from the spout of each*

34

> *bottle on the bar.* SARAH *has headed for the coffee table, where she pops a brownie into her mouth*)

HARRY   I'll turn out the lights.

SARAH (*With mouth very full*)   I will! (HARRY *points and gives her that "I-caught-you" look*) I always do.

HARRY   No, you don't.

SARAH   Oh, Harry, I love you.

> (*She leaves.* HARRY *goes over to steal a drink out of* ROBERT'S *old glass*)

ROBERT (*From the other side of the stage, having observed the previous scene*)   Harry? (HARRY *looks up*) You ever sorry you got married?

HARRY (*Sings "Sorry-Grateful"*)
You're always sorry,
You're always grateful,
You're always wondering what might have been.
Then she walks in.

> (SARAH *has entered to clear the coffee table*)

And still you're sorry,
And still you're grateful,
And still you wonder and still you doubt,
And she goes out.

> (SARAH *leaves with the coffee service*)

Everything's different,
Nothing's changed,

Only maybe slightly
Rearranged.
You're sorry-grateful,
Regretful-happy.
Why look for answers where none occur?
You always are what you always were,
Which has nothing to do with,
All to do with her.

SARAH (*Offstage*) Harry, darling, come to bed.

HARRY Coming, darling.

> (*He stands still.* ROBERT *looks up as* DAVID *appears in his apartment and begins to sing*)

DAVID
You're always sorry,
You're always grateful,
You hold her thinking, "I'm not alone."
You're still alone.
You don't live for her,
You do live with her,
You're scared she's starting to drift away
And scared she'll stay.

LARRY (*Appears in his apartment and sings*)
Good things get better,
Bad get worse.
Wait—I think I meant that in reverse.

HARRY, DAVID and LARRY
You're sorry-grateful,
Regretful-happy,
Why look for answers where none occur?

You'll always be what you always were,
Which has nothing to do with,
All to do with her.

(DAVID *leaves*)

HARRY and LARRY
You'll always be what you always were,
Which has nothing to do with,
All to do with her.

(LARRY *leaves*)

HARRY
Nothing to do with,
All to do with her.

(*The lights fade on him.* ROBERT *takes an elevator to a terrace overlooking the city.*)

The scene is PETER *and* SUSAN's *terrace. He is an Ivy League fellow, and she is a pretty, wide-eyed Southern lady.*

PETER (*Offstage*) Bob, Bob, where are you? (*Finding* ROBERT *on the terrace, and joining him*) What are you doing out here?

ROBERT It is so great to have a terrace. Wow.

SUSAN (*Coming out on the terrace; stepping over the clutter*) We never use it. We keep things like old sleds and stuff out here.

ROBERT You don't ever just sit out here?

PETER I hate it. And the kids are impossible out here. And everyone can hear everything you say. (*Yelling up to the floors above*) Are you listening? And it's dirty all the time. And look at all the bird-do.

(*He points to the railing where* ROBERT *has put his coat.* ROBERT *quickly removes it*)

SUSAN And noisy. Oo, that traffic. You can't even hear yourself think. And what can you see? It's not like you see something. You just see the building across the street.

PETER Well, if you lean way out and look over there you can see the East River.

(All three lean over the railing)

SUSAN   *(Nervously pulling them back)*   Except we decided you really can't. Peter almost met his Maker one night trying to see that old East River. He did.

ROBERT   You saved him?

SUSAN   Me? No. Well—in a way.

PETER   She fainted. So I got down.

SUSAN   Peter just is not afraid of anything at all. Unfortunately, I was not made that way. One day Peter fell off the ladder when he was putting up my curio cabinet and he split his head right open. Well, I fainted. I came to, I looked at his head and I fainted again. Four times I fainted that night.

ROBERT *(Laughing)*   Well, that is sweet. I mean you're a woman. I think that is very charming. Very. I do. In fact she is, without a doubt, the most charming woman I have ever, ever met. You are a lucky guy, Peter. *(Gives her a little hug)* I mean, that kind of—oh, Southern graciousness—there just ain't no more of that around. You two are beautiful together. Really. And Peter—if you ever decide to leave her I want to be the first to know.

SUSAN *(Smiles at PETER)*   Well . . .

PETER   You're the first to know.

ROBERT   What?

SUSAN *(Excitedly)*   We're getting divorced.

PETER   We haven't told anyone yet.

ROBERT *(Stunned; pauses)*   Oh! *(The music of "Bobby Baby" is heard in the orchestra)* I'm—uh—so surprised. *(They just smile at him. They don't speak)* Maybe you'll work it out. *(He gets no reaction. The music of "Bobby Baby" is heard again)* Don't think so, huh? Well, I know how hard it is for you and how you must feel . . .

(The lights fade on the terrace as ROBERT takes the elevator down to DAVID and JENNY'S apartment)

40

JENNY *and* DAVID, *staring straight ahead, are seated in their den, which also seems to serve as their children's playroom.* ROBERT *enters and sits near* JENNY. JENNY *directs much of this opening conversation to* DAVID, *who doesn't respond, but smiles increasingly.*

JENNY (*Very rapidly, answering* ROBERT's *last line from the previous scene*) Feel? I just don't feel anything. David, I don't care for any more. (*Hands him the butt of a joint.* DAVID, *staring straight ahead, caught up in his own euphoria, takes the butt and, as if by rote, extinguishes it in an ashtray*) It's too small. That's too small. It probably just doesn't work on me. Do you feel anything, David? Do you, honey? Because I don't.

ROBERT You will.

JENNY *When?* I mean, we've had *two,* for heavensake. I think maybe it depends on the person's constitution. Don't you, Dave? Well, listen, it's always good to try everything once.

(DAVID *doesn't respond*)

ROBERT Just wait!

JENNY I'm not planning to go anywhere. Maybe I'm just too dumb or square, but I honestly don't feel anything.

Do you, Dave? Because I don't. Absolutely nothing.
Honestly, not a thing. I mean, I *wish* I did. I just don't.
Maybe they gave you *real* grass, right off the front lawn.
I knew I wouldn't feel anything, though. I don't have
that kind of constitution. Why am I talking so much?

ROBERT   You're stoned.

JENNY   Am I? Am I? I am not.

DAVID (*Gives a short chortle; then*)   I am.

JENNY   Are you? You are not. I'm so dry!

ROBERT   You're stoned.

JENNY   Is that part of it?

ROBERT   You'll probably get hungry too.

JENNY   Yes? Should I feel *that*, too?

ROBERT   You don't have to feel anything.

JENNY   Are you hungry, Dave?

DAVID   No. I'd like some water, though.

JENNY   Me, too. (*She gets up to get a pitcher of water*)
Do you want some, Robert?

ROBERT   No, thank you.

JENNY (*She stops and turns back to* ROBERT)   What?

ROBERT   I don't want any, Jenny, thank you.

JENNY   Any what, Robert?

DAVID   You asked him, honey. Water!

JENNY   Oh, water . . . I could not remember what we were talking about.

ROBERT   See, you forget when you're high!

JENNY   Ohhh, God, do you. Wow. Are you high, Dave?

DAVID   I'm potted.

JENNY (*Sits down again, laughing*)   Potted. That is beautiful. Jesus!

ROBERT   You're really high now, huh?

JENNY   Jesus!

DAVID   That's twice you said "Jesus."

JENNY   You're kidding.

DAVID   No. You said it two times. She never swears.

JENNY   I didn't even know I said it once.

DAVID   Say "son-of-a-bitch."

JENNY   Son-of-a-bitch.

(*They all laugh so riotously that* DAVID *falls out of his chair*)

DAVID (*From the floor*)   Say "Kiss my ass."

JENNY   Kiss my ass. (*They roar at this, and* JENNY *tumbles to the floor near* DAVID *and they hug each other*) Kiss my ass, you son of a bitch. (*They all scream with laughter. Now* ROBERT *falls to the floor*) Oh, Jesus. (*She yells*) That's three!

A VOICE (*Offstage*)   Will you shut up—down there! It's two o'clock, for Chrissakes!

JENNY   Shhh, oh, shhh. Laugh to yourselves.

(*She quiets them down and almost tiptoes to the direction of the voice. Then she loudly yells in the same direction*) IT'S ALL RIGHT, NOW!

DAVID   Shhh, Jenny, for God's sake.

(ROBERT *starts laughing again*)

JENNY (*Comes back to them*)   Bobby, stop! We'll get evicted.

ROBERT   Jenny, you're terrific. You're the girl I should have married.

(*The laughter subsides a bit*)

JENNY   Listen, I know a darling girl in this building you'll just love.

ROBERT   What?

JENNY   When are you going to get married?

DAVID   What?

JENNY   I mean it. To me a person's not complete until he's married.

44

ROBERT   Oh, I will. It's not like I'm avoiding marriage. It's avoiding me, if anything. I'm ready.

JENNY   Actually, you're not. But listen, not everybody should be married, I guess.

DAVID   I don't know. See, to me, a man should be married. Your life has a—what? What am I trying to say? A point to it—a bottom, you know what I'm saying? I have everything, but freedom. Which is everything, huh? No. (*Takes* JENNY's *hand*) *This* is everything. I got my wife, my kids, a home. I feel that—uh—well, you gotta give up to get. Know what I'm saying?

ROBERT   Listen, I agree. But you know what bothers me— is, if you marry, then you've got another person *there* all the time. Plus you can't get out of it, whenever you just might want to get out of it. You are caught! See? And even if you do get out of it, what do you have to show for it? Not to mention the fact that—then—you've always been married. I mean, you can never not have been married again.

JENNY   I don't feel you're really ready. Do you think, just maybe, I mean, subconsciously—you might be resisting it?

ROBERT   No. Negative. Absolutely not! I meet girls all the time. All over the place. All you have to do is live in New York and you meet a girl a minute. Right now, I date this stewardess, cute, original . . . (APRIL *appears with the "Bobby Baby" music*) . . . odd. And Kathy, you never met Kathy, did you? Well, she's the best . . . (KATHY *appears*) . . . just the best! And then there's Marta. (MARTA *appears*) God, she's fun! I'm certainly not resisting marriage! (*The three girls react to this in absolute disbelief*) My life is totally prepared for a gigantic change right now. I'm ready to be married.

DAVID Right. Then, why aren't you?

ROBERT Right.

MARTA Right.

APRIL Right.

KATHY Right.

APRIL, KATHY and MARTA (*Sing "You Could Drive a Person Crazy"*)

> Doo-doo-doo-doo
> Doo-doo-doo-doo
> Doo-doo-doo-doo-doo-doo
> You could drive a person crazy,
> You could drive a person mad.
> Doo-doo doo-doo doo
> First you make a person hazy
> So a person could be had.
> Doo-doo doo-doo doo
> Then you leave a person dangling sadly
> Outside your door.
> Which it only makes a person gladly
> Want you even more,
> I could understand a person
> If it's not a person's bag.
> Doo-doo doo-doo doo
> I could understand a person
> If a person was a fag.
> Doo-doo doo-doo doo
> Boo-boo-boo-boo
> But worse 'n that,

A person that
Titillates a person and then leaves her flat
Is crazy,
He's a troubled person,
He's a truly crazy person
Himself!

You crummy bastard! You son-of-a-bitch!

Bobby is my hobby and I'm giving it up.

KATHY

When a person's personality is personable,
He shouldn't oughta sit like a lump.
It's harder than a matador coercin' a bull
To try to get you off-a your rump.
So single and attentive and attractive a man
Is everything a person could wish,
But turning off a person is the act of a man
Who likes to pull the hooks out of fish.

APRIL, KATHY and MARTA

Knock, knock, is anybody there?
Knock, knock, it really isn't fair.
Knock, knock, I'm working all my charms.
Knock, knock, a zombie's in my arms.
All that sweet affection,
What is wrong?
Where's the loose connection?
How long, oh Lord, how long?
Bobby baby, Bobby bubi, Bobby,

You could drive a person buggy,
You could blow a person's cool.
Doo-doo doo-doo doo
Like you make a person feel all huggy

While you make her feel a fool.
Doo-doo doo-doo doo
When a person says that you've upset her
That's when you're good.
You impersonate a person better
Than a zombie should.

I could understand a person
If he wasn't good in bed.
Doo-doo-doo-doo doo
I could understand a person
If he actually was dead.
Doo-doo-doo-doo
Exclusive you,
Elusive you,
Will any person ever get the juice of you?
You're crazy,
You're a lovely person,
You're a moving, deeply maladjusted,
Never to be trusted
Crazy person
Yourself.

(After a bow to the audience, they exit)

JENNY   I'm starving. I'll get us something to eat. *(Gets up)* Do one of you sons-of-bitches want to help? Then kiss my ass.

(She laughs)

DAVID *(Strangely serious, not looking at* JENNY*)*   Oh, boy.

(He lights a cigarette and moves away)

JENNY   Did you light another one?

DAVID Just a cigarette.

ROBERT Shall I roll another one?

JENNY Maybe one.

DAVID No.

ROBERT I can roll another one in a second.

DAVID No.

JENNY No more?

DAVID (*A moment. Then looks at* JENNY) I don't think so.

JENNY (*After a pause*) I don't think so either.

ROBERT It'll just take a second to make another one.

(*There is a long pause*)

DAVID Listen, you two have one.

JENNY I don't want one.

DAVID Have one if you want one.

JENNY But I don't (*A pause*) I'll get some food. (*She embraces* DAVID) Isn't he a marvelous man?

DAVID (*Lovingly*) I married a square. A confessed square.

JENNY (*She starts to go, then turns seriously to* ROBERT) Bobby, we're just too old! We were all—trying to keep up with the kids tonight. Goodness, we've *been* there already. Who wants to go back? But, anyway, what do I know?

DAVID   Hey, screwball. I'm starving.

JENNY   I love you . . . so much.

DAVID   Food!

JENNY   And, Bobby—put that stuff away. C'mon, put it in your pocket. Take it home. Come on. (ROBERT *does so*) Thank you. I don't know. Maybe you're right. Who ever knows?

(*She smiles and goes out*)

ROBERT   (*Not happy*)   What was all that?

DAVID   She doesn't go for it. I thought she wouldn't go for it.

ROBERT   (*Cold*)   She was stoned.

DAVID   Not really. She doesn't get things like that. I mean, she'll go along with it, but that's about it.

ROBERT   (*Colder*)   She didn't like it?

DAVID   I know her. She didn't.

ROBERT   (*Pauses*)   You want me to get *you* some?

DAVID   She'd have a fit. I'm really surprised she did it tonight.

ROBERT   She loved it.

DAVID (*Correcting* ROBERT)   For *me*. She loved it for me.
She didn't really love it. I know her. She's what she said
. . . square . . . dumb . . .

ROBERT   Like a fox.

(*The music of "Bobby Baby" is heard in the orchestra*)

DAVID (*After a pause of staring at each other*)   I'll go see
if I can give her a hand. What do you say?

(*He exits*)

ROBERT (*Watching him go*)   Wow! Oh, wow!

(*He starts to leave but is stopped by all the couples,
who begin to appear in their apartments, as in the
opening number*)

ALL
Bobby, Bobby, Bobby baby,
Bobby bubi, Robby, Robert darling,
Bobby, we've been trying to reach you.
Angel, I've got something to tell you . . .
Bobby, it's important or I wouldn't call . . .
Whatcha doing Thursday?
Bobby, look, I know how you hate it and all . . .
But this is something special.
Bobby, come on over for dinner.
There's someone we want you to meet.
Bobby, come on over for dinner . . .
This girl from the office . . .

My niece from Ohio . . .
It'll just be the four of us . .
You'lll loooooooooooooove her!

(*The wives exit and the husbands now sing "Have I Got a Girl for You?"*)

LARRY

Have I got a girl for you? Wait till you meet her!
Have I got a girl for you, boy? Hoo, boy!
Dumb!—and with a weakness for Sazerac slings—
You give her even the fruit and she swings.
The kind of girl you can't send through the mails—
Call me tomorrow, I want the details.

PETER

Have I got a chick for you? Wait till you meet her!
Have I got a chick for you, boy? Hoo, boy!
Smart!—She's into all those exotic mystiques:
The Kamasutra and Chinese techniques—
I hear she knows more than seventy-five . . .
Call me tomorrow if you're still alive.

HUSBANDS (*In canon*)

Have I got a girl for you? Wait till you meet her!
Have I got a girl for you, boy? Hoo, boy!
Boy, to be in your shoes what I wouldn't give.
I mean the freedom to go out and live . . .
And as for settling down and all that . . .
Marriage may be where it's been, but it's not where
   it's at!

Whaddaya like, you like coming home to a kiss?
Somebody with a smile at the door?
Whaddaya like, you like indescribable bliss?
Then whaddaya wanna get married for?

Whaddya like, you like an excursion to Rome,
Suddenly taking off to explore?
Whaddaya like, you like having meals cooked at
  home?
Then whaddaya wanna get married for?
Whaddaya wanna get married for?
Whaddaya wanna get married for?
Whaddaya wanna get married for?

(*The husbands exit, leaving* ROBERT *alone onstage.
He now sings "Someone is Waiting." Throughout
the song as each wife is mentioned, she appears with
her husband, intimately in their own apartment*)

ROBERT
Someone is waiting,
Cool as Sarah,
Easy and loving as Susan—
Jenny.
Someone is waiting,
Warm as Susan,
Frantic and touching as Amy—
Joanne.

Would I know her even if I met her?
Have I missed her? Did I let her go?
A Susan sort of Sarah,
A Jennyish Joanne,
Wait for me, I'm ready now,
I'll find you if I can!

Someone will hold me,
Soft as Jenny,
Skinny and blue-eyed as Amy—
Susan.
Someone will wake me,

Sweet as Amy,
Tender and foolish as Sarah—
Joanne.

Did I know her? have I waited too long?
Maybe so, but maybe so has she,
My blue-eyed Sarah
Warm Joanne
Sweet Jenny
Loving Susan
Crazy Amy,
Wait for me,
I'll hurry, wait for me.
Hurry.
Wait for me.
Hurry.
Wait for me.

(*The lights dim on the couples.* ROBERT *is left standing alone*)

The lights come up on a girl, MARTA, *who is seated on a park bench on stage level.* ROBERT *sits on the other end of the bench. She sings "Another Hundred People."*

MARTA

Another hundred people just got off of the train
And came up through the ground
While another hundred people just got off of the bus
And are looking around
At another hundred people who got off of the plane
And are looking at us
Who got off of the train
And the plane and the bus
Maybe yesterday.

It's a city of strangers—
Some come to work, some to play—
A city of strangers—
Some come to stare, some to stay,
And every day
The ones who stay
Can find each other in the crowded streets and the
    guarded parks,
By the rusty fountains and the dusty trees with the
    battered barks,
And they walk together past the postered walls with
    the crude remarks,

And they meet at parties through the friends of friends
who they never know.
Will you pick me up or do I meet you there or shall we
let it go?
Did you get my message? 'Cause I looked in vain.
Can we see each other Tuesday if it doesn't rain?
Look, I'll call you in the morning or my service will
explain . . .

And another hundred people just got off of the train.

(APRIL, *in an airline stewardess' uniform, enters and
sits next to* ROBERT. MARTA, *although she is not in-
cluded, listens to the scene*)

APRIL   I didn't come right to New York. I went to Northwestern University for two years, but it was a pitiful
mistake. I was on probation the whole two years. I was
getting ready to go back to Shaker Heights when I
decided where I really wanted to live more than any other
place was—Radio City. I thought it was a wonderful
little city near New York. So I came here. I'm very dumb.

ROBERT   You're not dumb, April.

APRIL   To me I am. Even the reason I stayed in New York
was because I just cannot get interested in myself—I'm
so boring.

ROBERT   I find you very interesting.

APRIL   Well, I'm just not. I used to think I was so odd.
But my roommate is the same way. He's also very dumb.

ROBERT   Oh, you never mentioned him. Is he—your lover?

56

APRIL   Oh, no. We just share this great big apartment on
West End Avenue. We have our own rooms and everything. I'd show it to you but we've never had company.
He's the sweetest thing, actually. I think he likes the
arrangement. I don't know, though—we never discuss it.
He was born in New York, so *nothing* really interests
him. I don't have anything more to say.

(She exits)

MARTA *(Sings)*

And they find each other in the crowded streets and
the guarded parks,
By the rusty fountains and the dusty trees with the
battered barks,
And they walk together past the postered walls with
the crude remarks,
And they meet at parties through the friends of friends
who they never know.
Will you pick me up or do I meet you there or shall
we let it go?
Did you get my message? 'Cause I looked in vain.
Can we see each other Tuesday if it doesn't rain?
Look, I'll call you in the morning or my service will
explain . . .

And another hundred people just got off of the train.

*(Now KATHY enters and sits next to ROBERT on the
bench)*

KATHY   See, Bobby, some people have to know when to
come to New York, and some people have to know when
to leave. I always thought I'd just naturally come here
and spend the rest of my life here. I wanted to have two

57

terrific affairs and then get married. I always knew I was meant to be a wife.

ROBERT   You should have asked me.

KATHY   Wanna marry me?

ROBERT   I did. I honestly did . . . in the beginning. But I . . . I don't know. I never thought that you ever would.

KATHY   I would. I never understood why you'd never ask me.

ROBERT (*Puts his arm around her*)   You wanted to marry me? And I wanted to marry you. Well then, how the hell did we ever end up such good friends?

KATHY   Bobby, I'm moving to Vermont.

ROBERT   Vermont? Why Vermont?

KATHY   That's where *he* lives. I'm getting married.

ROBERT (*A pause; takes his arm away*)   What?

KATHY   Some people still get married, you know.

ROBERT   Do you love him?

KATHY   I'll be a good wife. I just don't want to run around this city any more like I'm having a life. (*She pauses*) As I said before, some people have to know when to come to New York and some people have to know when to leave.

(*And she's gone.* MARTA *continues singing*)

MARTA

Another hundred people just got off of the train
And came up through the ground
While another hundred people just got off of the bus
And are looking around
At another hundred people who got off of the plane
And are looking at us
Who got off of the train
And the plane and the bus
Maybe yesterday.

It's a city of strangers—
Some come to work, some to play—
A city of strangers—
Some come to stare, some to stay,
And every day
Some go away.
   (*She looks off in the direction in which* KATHY *has gone*)
Or they find each other in the crowded streets and the
   guarded parks,
By the rusty fountains and the dusty trees with the
   battered barks,
And they walk together past the postered walls with
   the crude remarks,
And they meet at parties through the friends of friends
   who they never know.
Will you pick me up or do I meet you there or shall
   we let it go?
Did you get my message? 'Cause I looked in vain.
Can we see each other Tuesday if it doesn't rain?
Look, I'll call you in the morning or my service will
   explain . . .

And another hundred people just got off of the train.

And another hundred people just got off of the train.
And another hundred people just got off of the train.
And another hundred people just got off of the train.
And another hundred people just got off of the train.

(*She turns to* ROBERT)

You wanna know why I came to New York? I came because New York is the center of the world and that's where I want to be. You know what the pulse of this city is?

ROBERT   A busy signal?

MARTA   The pulse of this city, kiddo, is *me*. This city is for the me's of this world. People that want to be right in the heart of it. *I* am the soul of New York.

ROBERT   How 'bout that.

MARTA   See, smart remarks do not a person make. How many Puerto Ricans do you know?

ROBERT   I'm not sure.

MARTA   How many blacks?

ROBERT   Well, very few, actually. I seem to meet people only like myself.

MARTA   (*Gives* ROBERT *a look*)   Talk about your weirdos . . . *I* pass people on the streets and I know them. Every son-of-a-bitch is my friend. I go uptown to the dentist or something, and I suddenly want to cry because I think, "Oh my God, I'm *up*town." And Fourteenth Street. Well, nobody knows it, but *that* is the center of the universe.

60

ROBERT   Fourteenth Street?

MARTA   That's humanity, Fourteenth Street. That's everything. And if you don't like it there they got every subway
you can name to take you where you like it better.

ROBERT   God bless Fourteenth Street.

MARTA   This city—I kiss the ground of it. Someday, you
know what I want to do? I want to get all dressed up
in black—black dress, black shoes, hat, everything black,
and go sit in some bar, at the end of the counter, and
drink and cry. That is my idea of honest-to-God sophisti-
cation. I mean, *that's* New York. (*Pauses*) You always
make me feel like I got the next line. What is it with you?

ROBERT   I just never met anybody like you.

MARTA   Me neither. You know what this city is? Where
a person can feel it? It's in a person's ass. If you're really
part of this city, relaxed, cool and in the whole flow of
it, your ass is like this. (*She makes a large round circle
with her forefinger and thumb*) If you're just living
here, running around uptight, not really part of this
city, your ass is like this.

(*She tightens the circle to nothing*)

ROBERT   I . . . hesitate to ask. (*She holds up the "tight"
sign high and abruptly. As the lights start to dim we
hear*) That's a fascinating theory. Indeed fascinating.
And at this moment, extraordinarily accurate.

(*The lights fade to a blackout*)

SCENE SIX

A girl in a white choir robe appears on an upper level as AMY's *kitchen comes into view on stage level.* AMY, *in a white wedding dress, is seated at the counter, nervously shining a pair of black men's shoes. There are coats and umbrellas hanging on a wall rack.*

CHOIRGIRL *(Sings softly to organ accompaniment)*
    Bless this day, pinnacle of life,
    Husband joined to wife,
    The heart leaps up to behold
    This golden day.

PAUL *(Appears in a dress shirt, shorts and socks)* Amy, I can't find my shoes any . . .

    (Sees AMY *with his shoes, stops and sings to her adoringly)*

Today is for Amy,
Amy, I give you the rest of my life.
To cherish and to keep you,
To honor you forever,
Today is for Amy,
My happily soon-to-be wife.

Amy, we're really getting married!

    (He goes out. She shakes her head "yes" and it becomes "no")

AMY (*Looking at the audience, sings*)
> Pardon me, is everybody there?
> Because if everybody's
> There I want to thank you all for coming to the
> wedding. I'd ap-
> Preciate your going even more, I mean, you must have
> lots of
> Better things to do. And not a word of it to Paul.
> Remember
> Paul? You know, the man I'm gonna marry, but I'm
> not because I
> Wouldn't ruin anyone as wonderful as he is—
>
> Thank you all
> For the gifts and the flowers.
> Thank you all,
> Now it's back to the showers.
> Don't tell Paul,
> But I'm not getting married today.
> > (*In choir robes, members of the company join the*
> > CHOIRGIRL *on the upper level and hum*)

CHOIRGIRL
> Bless this day, tragedy of life,
> Husband joined to wife.
> The heart sinks down and feels dead
> This dreadful day.

ROBERT (*Enters, dressed as the best man*)   Amy, Paul can't
find his good cuff links.

AMY   On the dresser! Right next to my suicide note.
> (ROBERT *leaves*)
>
> Listen everybody, look, I don't know what you're
> waiting for—a

Wedding, what's a wedding? It's a prehistoric ritual
    where
Everybody promises fidelity forever, which is
Maybe the most horrifying word I ever heard, and
    which is
Followed by a honeymoon, where suddenly he'll re-
    alize he's
Saddled with a nut and wanna kill me and he should.

Thanks a bunch,
But I'm not getting married.
Go have lunch,
'Cause I'm not getting married.
You've been grand,
But I'm not getting married.
Don't just stand there,
I'm not getting married.
And don't tell Paul
But I'm not getting married today!

Go! Can't you go?
Why is nobody listening?
Goodbye! Go and cry
At another person's wake.
If you're quick, for a kick
You could pick up a christening,
But please, on my knees,
There's a human life at stake.

Listen everybody, I'm afraid you didn't hear, or do you
Want to see a crazy lady fall apart in front of you? It
Isn't only Paul who may be ruining his life, you know,
    we'll
Both of us be losing our identities—I telephoned my

Analyst about it but he said to see him Monday, and by
Monday I'll be floating in the Hudson, with the other
  garbage.

I'm not well,
So I'm not getting married.
You've been swell,
But I'm not getting married.
Clear the hall
'Cause I'm not getting married.
Thank you all
But I'm not getting married.
And don't tell Paul,
But I'm not getting married today!

(*More members of the company, dressed in choir
robes, enter in a wedding-march, now forming a
complete choir*)

CHOIRGIRL
Bless this bride, totally insane,
Slipping down the drain,

(*Sound of thunder*)

And bless this day in our hearts—

(*Sound of rain*)

As it starts to rain . . .

(*Members of the* CHOIR *open up umbrellas of different colors.* PAUL *reenters, fully dressed in his
tuxedo now*)

PAUL	AMY
Today is for Amy.	Go, can't you go?
Amy—	Look, you know
I give you	I adore you all,
The rest of my life,	But why watch me die
To cherish	Like Eliza on the ice?
And to keep	Look, perhaps
You,	I'll collapse
To honor you	In the apse right
Forever.	Before you all,
Today is for	So take back the cake,
Amy,	Burn the shoes and boil
My happily	the rice.
Soon-to-be	Look, I didn't want to
Wife.	have to tell you,
	But I may be coming
	down with hepatitis
	And I think I'm gonna
	faint,
	So if you wanna see
	me faint,
	I'll do it happily,
	But wouldn't it be funnier
	To go and watch a
	funeral?
	So thank you for the
	Twenty-seven dinner
	plates and
	Thirty-seven butter
	knives and
	Forty-seven paper-
My	weights and
Adorable	Fifty-seven candle-
Wife—	holders . . .

66

One more thing,	I am not getting married	CHOIR
Softly said,	But I'm not getting married	Amen
"With this ring	Still I'm not getting married	Amen
I thee wed."	See, I'm not getting married	Amen
Let us pray,	Let us pray,	Amen
And we are	That I'm not	Amen
Getting married today!	Getting married today!	

(ROBERT enters with the ring. AMY gets very busy preparing breakfast with toast, dishes, glasses, etc.)

PAUL   Amy?

AMY   You're starting! (*He begins to speak*) Don't talk, please! Why don't the two of you sit down and talk to each other? I can't think with the two of you following me—every place I go—from the bedroom to the bathroom to the kitchen . . . I feel like I'm leading a parade (*The two men sit down at the counter*) Paul, stop staring! I feel it—like bullets—right through my back. (*Without stopping*) No, Paul, please! (*Pouring orange juice*) I'm so crazy I left the refrigerator door open last night, so the orange juice is hot. (*Hands PAUL his juice*) Here, and if you say "thank you" I will go running right out of this apartment and move into the Hopeless Cases Section at Bellevue, where they'll understand me. Don't talk, please. (*Suddenly, from behind his chair, she throws her arms around his neck and kisses him all over his head, finally pressing her face against his*) Oh, Paul. I apologize. Oh, Paul, you say whatever you want to say. Whatever you like. Who am *I* telling *you* what to do? Oh, Paul.

PAUL (*Pauses*)   The orange juice is hot. But thanks.

AMY   Paul, see! You don't thank a person for hot orange juice! You slug 'em. (*Smoke is billowing out of the toaster*) The toast! Now I blew the toast.

(*She flips up two charred pieces of toast*)

PAUL   That's okay.

AMY   I can't stand it! (*Scraping the burned toast*) IT'S NOT OKAY, PAUL. NOTHING ABOUT IT EVEN REMOTELY RESEMBLES OKAY. IT IS THE OPPOSITE OF OKAY. Oh, Robert, this is the real me. Crazed!

ROBERT (*Teasing, hesitantly*)   I was just thinking that this is probably a much more interesting wedding breakfast than most. And—uh—that the bride certainly has a lot of energy! The groom is abnormally quiet. But yet a festive atmosphere pervades the room—I guess it's the best man, smiling, even as he dies from drinking boiled orange juice.

(*He holds up his orange juice in a mock toast*)

AMY   I would laugh, Robert, if it weren't all so tragic. (*To PAUL*) How do I look? Funny?

PAUL   Yeah, that's a funny dress.

(*He starts pouring the coffee*)

AMY   That dumb hairdresser straightened my hair like he was on withdrawal. Paul, what are you so happy about all the time?

PAUL You.

(*He hands her a cup and saucer*)

AMY This is the most neurotic . . . insane . . . it is . . . so *crazy* having this enormous wedding and everything after we've been living together all these years! It's embarrassing, Paul. People will think I'm pregnant.

PAUL That's next year. Listen, if we hurry we're late.

AMY What am I doing? I'm thirty-one.

PAUL And perfect.

AMY Oh, an oldie but a goodie, huh? It's just incredible. Two years with a psychiatrist . . . and look where it leads. I am just so glad we're not having a Catholic wedding because next year when I get the divorce I won't be a sinner. Whoever would have thought I'd *marry* someone Jewish? Jewish! I mean I didn't even *know* anybody who was Jewish. See, Robert. That was probably my main attraction. Look what a little Catholic rebellion will lead to! The very first moment I met Paul, I said to myself, "That's what I really like—that Jew!" Oh, he was so beautiful . . . inside and out beautiful. Paul would kiss me and I would think, "Oh, I got my very own Jew!"

PAUL What is all this about me being Jewish today? About three-quarters of your friends are Jewish. Hurry.

AMY Did I ever say I like my friends? I do not. I much prefer my gentile enemies—at least they leave you alone. And I need to be left alone. I'm just like Robert.

ROBERT (*Outraged*)   I'm not like *that*! What the hell are you talking about? But don't answer, because we don't have time.

PAUL   Amy. After all these years, don't you know we fit?

AMY   The higher you go, the harder you hurt when you fall.

PAUL (*So gentle*)   I never dropped you yet.

(*About to cry, she goes to take a sip of coffee, sees a note in the saucer, looks to* PAUL, *and then shows the saucer to* ROBERT. ROBERT *opens the note*)

ROBERT   "Whoever reads this . . . I love you." Well, thank you, I love *you*.

AMY   Thank *him*. The phantom. He leaves notes like that all over the place. A person can't stand all that sweetness, Paul. Nobody human can stand all that everlasting affection.

PAUL   Amy, don't you think we should go?

AMY (*There is nothing more for her to do*)   I can't.

PAUL   Amy, if anybody should be married, it's you. Tell her, Robert.

AMY   Robert tell me? Who's going to tell Robert?

ROBERT (*He pauses; then, right at* PAUL)   Paul, I can't tell anybody anything like that. I guess whatever is right will happen.

PAUL (*Pauses*)   I see.

ROBERT   Listen, I'm going to call and say that, ah . . . that
. . . that we'll be late. That we'll be a little late. The
people will be getting there, don't you think?

(ROBERT *goes out*)

PAUL   Amy, do you see what you're doing to yourself? Do
you know if other people did to you what you do to
yourself, they could be put in jail? C'mon.

(*Thunder is heard*)

AMY   Oh, Paul, look . . . oh, look . . . it's starting to rain.

ROBERT (*Entering*)   It's starting to rain. The line's busy.
(*He tries to be light*) Oh, guess who I ran into coming
over here today. Helen Kincaid. Remember Helen
Kincaid? I brought her around a few times. Well, she's
married now. I almost didn't recognize her, all fat and
blowzy and . . .

(*He realizes what he is saying*)

PAUL (*Softly*)   Amy, c'mon. We're late.

AMY   I can't do it, Paul. I don't understand how I ever let
it get this far. (*Thunder is heard again*) Oh, look, will
you look at that, now it's really starting to rain . . . Look
at it . . . It's a flood, it's a sign—thank you, God, now
explain it to him!

PAUL (*Quietly*)   Amy, let's go. All our friends are waiting.

AMY   That's no reason, Paul. I just can't. I'm so afraid.

7 1

PAUL Of what?

AMY (*She is crying*) I don't know. I don't know. I just think you're really not for me, Paul. I just think maybe nobody's for me. I never saw one good marriage. Never. Not in my entire life.

PAUL You just see what you look for, you know. I've seen a lot. Listen, Amy, married people are no more *marriage* than . . . oh . . . musicians are music. Just because some of the people might be wrong doesn't matter . . . *it* is still *right*.

AMY Yes, well, I'll put that on a sampler, Paul. (*She looks up—right at* PAUL) Please. I'm not being emotional. I'm as sane as can be. Paul? I'm sorry. I don't love you enough.

> (*There is a very long pause as they stare at each other*)

PAUL (*He fights for control. He speaks hesitantly, yet his voice still trembles*) Robert . . . would you . . . call and, ah, explain and . . . I'm . . . I, ah, I . . .

> (*He goes out quickly*)

AMY (*She doesn't move; drained of emotion, really asking . . .*) What did I just do?

ROBERT (*Reflectively*) You did . . . what you had to do, I guess . . . If it was right, you would have gone through with it. That's what I think, anyway . . . (*A pause*) Amy, marry *me*.

AMY What?

ROBERT Marry me.

> (*The music of "Bobby Baby" is heard in the orchestra*)

AMY *Huh?*

ROBERT You said it before—we're just alike. Why don't we, Amy?

AMY Why don't we, Robert?

VOICES (*Offstage*)
Bobby, Bobby,
Bobby baby, Bobby bubi,
Robby . . .

ROBERT Marry me! And everybody'll leave us alone!

VOICES (*Offstage*)
Bobby . . . Bobby . . . How have you been?
Stop by on your way home . . .
Bobby, we've been thinking of you!

AMY Isn't this some world? I'm afraid to get married, and you're afraid not to. Thank you, Robert. I'm really . . . it's just that you have to want to marry *some*body, not just some*body*.

> (*She hugs him*)

VOICES (*Offstage*)
Bobby, come on over for dinner!
Just be the three of us,
Only the three of us,
We LOOOOOOOOOOOOOVE . . .

(*Thunder interrupts the voices.* AMY *notices the raincoats*)

AMY Oh! Would you look at that! He went out without an umbrella or anything. (*She puts on a raincoat, and grabs another coat and umbrella for* PAUL) He'll get pneumonia. I've got to catch him. I'm getting married. Oh, and he's so good, isn't he? So good.

(*She starts to leave*)

ROBERT Amy!

(*He picks up the bouquet and throws it to her*)

AMY I'm the next bride.

(*She leaves. The kitchen slides off*)

VOICES (*Offstage*)
Bobby, Bobby,
Bobby baby, Bobby bubi,
Robby!

(*The lights come up on* ROBERT'*s apartment. All the birthday guests are looking at him as in* ACT ONE, SCENE ONE. ROBERT *stares at* AMY *as she enters with the cake and the music builds*)

Curtain

Act Two

ROBERT *is about to blow out the candles at the table, with all five couples standing there. As the scene progresses we find it to be more accelerated, isolating* ROBERT *at the end.*

AMY   Well, our blessings, Robert.

JENNY   Don't tell your wish, Bobby, or it won't come true.

(ROBERT *blows out most of the candles. The others blow out the rest hurriedly*)

JOANNE   You just blew it.

AMY   It probably was a wish you wouldn't have got anyway, Robert.

LARRY   You wish for a wife, Robert?

PETER   Don't. You're a lucky son-of-a-gun now. Hang in there.

SARAH   Stay exactly the same. You may be the one constant in this world of variables.

HARRY   I don't know, Sarah, you can't stay in your thirties forever.

JENNY   You'll still get your wish, Bobby.

JOANNE   Won't. I say he won't.

LARRY   Joanne, come on. See, when she and Robert get together . . .

JOANNE   Larry, I'm telling you, if you do not blow out all the candles on the cake, you do not get your wish. I know all the rules for birthday-candle blowing out. I've had enough for a wax museum.

ROBERT   All right, all right! Actually, I didn't wish for anything.

(*Again, each of the couples carries out a piece of* ROBERT's *furniture as the following lines are spoken*)

DAVID   What do you mean you didn't wish for . . .

SUSAN   Oh, tell, everybody's so curious.

PETER   Tell, but lie.

ROBERT   Thank you for including me in your thoughts, your lives . . .

HARRY   Stay exactly as you are, Robert.

SARAH   That's right, you sweet thing, you stay exactly as you are.

(*The music of* "Bobby Baby" *is heard from the orchestra*)

JOANNE   Everyone adores you. What an awful thing. I'd kiss you good night, Robby, but Larry gets s' jealous.

AMY Things always happen for the best. I don't even believe that myself.

> (*All have exited on their final lines, leaving* ROBERT *alone*)

ROBERT (*Shouting after them*) I mean, when you've got friends like mine . . . (*The music for "Side by Side by Side" begins*) I mean, when you've got friends like mine . . . (*He sings "Side by Side by Side"*)

Isn't it warm,
Isn't it rosy,
Side by side . . .

> (*The couples appear in their living areas and look at* ROBERT)

SARAH He's such a cutie.

ROBERT
. . . by side?

SARAH Isn't he a cutie?

ROBERT
Ports in a storm,
Comfy and cozy,
Side by side . . .

PETER He never loses his cool.

ROBERT
. . . by side . . .

HARRY I envy that.

(Robert starts up the stairs. Throughout the following lines, he wanders through each couple's living area, while the couples continue to refer to ROBERT *as if he were still standing center stage)*

ROBERT
>Everything shines,
>How sweet . . .

ROBERT, SARAH and HARRY
>Side by side . . .

SUSAN   We're just so fond of him.

ROBERT
>. . . by side,
>Parallel lines
>Who meet . . .

AMY, PAUL, PETER and SUSAN
>Love him—
>Can't get enough of him.

ROBERT
>Everyone winks,
>Nobody's nosy,
>Side by side . . .

JOANNE   He's just crazy about me.

ROBERT
>. . . by side.

PAUL   He's a very tender guy.

ROBERT
>You bring the drinks and
>I'll bring the posy . . .

ROBERT, LARRY and JOANNE
> Side by side . . .

LARRY   He's always there when you need him.

ROBERT
> . . . by side.
> One is lonely and two is boring,
> Think what you can keep ignoring,
> Side . . .

AMY   He's my best friend.

ROBERT
> . . . by side . . .

AMY (*Touching* PAUL)   Second best.

ROBERT
> . . . by side.

ALL (*Except* ROBERT)
> Never a bother,
> Seven times a godfather.

ROBERT, AMY and PAUL
> Year after year,
> Older and older . . .

LARRY   It's amazing. We've gotten older every year and he seems to stay exactly the same.

ALL
> Sharing a tear,
> Lending a shoulder . . .

DAVID   You know what comes to my mind when I see him? The Seagram Building. Isn't that funny?

ROBERT, PETER, SUSAN, SARAH and HARRY
Ain't we got fun?
No strain . . .

JOANNE Sometimes I catch him looking and looking. And
I just look right back.

(ROBERT *takes an elevator back to stage level*)

ALL
Permanent sun, no rain . . .
We're so crazy, he's so sane.

Friendship forbids
Anything bitter . . .

PAUL A person like Bob doesn't have the good things and
he doesn't have the bad things. But he doesn't have the
good things.

ALL
Being the kids
As well as the sitter . . .

HARRY Let me make him a drink. He's the only guy I
know, I feel should drink more.

ROBERT
One's impossible, two is dreary,
Three is company, safe and cheery,
ALL (*But* ROBERT *and* SARAH)
Side . . .

(*The couples leave their living areas.* ROBERT *is
alone onstage*)

SARAH   He always looks like he's keeping score.

ALL
   . . . by side . . .

SARAH   Who's winning, Robert?

ALL
   . . . by side.

ROBERT
   Here is the church,
   Here is the steeple,
   Open the doors and
   See all the crazy married people.

   (*The couples burst in all at once on stage level.
   The music continues directly into "What Would
   We Do Without You?"*)

ALL (*Except* ROBERT)
   What would we do without you?
   How would we ever get through?
   Who would I complain to for hours?
   Who'd bring me the flowers
   When I have the flu?
   Who'd finish yesterday's stew?
   Who'd take the kids to the zoo?
   Who is so dear?
   And who is so deep?
   And who would keep her/him occupied
   When I want to sleep?
   How would we ever get through?
   What would we do without you?

   What would we do without you?
   How would we ever get through?

Should there be a marital squabble,
Available Bob'll
Be there with the glue.
Who could we open up to,
Secrets we keep from guess-who?
Who is so safe and who is so sound?
You never need an analyst with Bobby around.
How could we ever get through?
What would we do without you?

What would we do without you?
How would we ever get through?
Who sends anniversary wishes?
Who helps with the dishes
And never says boo?
Who changes subjects on cue?
Who cheers us up when we're blue?
Who is a flirt but never a threat,
Reminds us of our birthdays, which we always forget?
How would we ever get through?
What would we do without you?

What would we do without you?
How would we ever get
How would we ever get
How would we ever get
How would we ever get . . . through?
What would we do without you?

ROBERT
Just what you usually do!
ALL (*Except* ROBERT)
Right!

You who sit with us,
You who share with us,
You who fit with us,

You who bear with us,
You-hoo, you-hoo, you-hoo,
You-hoo, you-hoo . . .

ROBERT (*In a vaudeville call*)   Okay, now everybody!

ALL
Isn't it warm, isn't it rosy,
Side by side?
Ports in a storm, comfy and cozy,
Side by side,
Everything shines, how sweet,
Side by side,
Parallel lines who meet
Side by side.
Year after year, older and older,
Side by side,
Sharing a tear and lending a shoulder,
Side by side.
Two's impossible, two is gloomy,
Give another number to me.
Side by side,
By side, by side, by side, by side,
By side, by side, by side, by side,
By side!

(*All the couples exit, leaving* ROBERT *alone onstage*)

The scene is ROBERT's *apartment.* APRIL *enters. She is
wearing her stewardess' uniform and appears self-conscious;
this is her first visit. The stage level is completely cleared.
(*APRIL *and* ROBERT *refer to furnishings that aren't there*)

APRIL   Oh! It's a darling apartment.

ROBERT   Thank you.

APRIL   Just darling. Did you do it yourself?

ROBERT   Me? Yes, I did, yes.

APRIL   Yourself?

ROBERT   Yes.

APRIL   Really?

ROBERT   Yes.

APRIL   Well, it's darling—Did you really do it all yourself?

ROBERT (*Getting tired of this*)   Yes! Why? Did you hear I
didn't?

APRIL   No, but look—this! This is just precious.

ROBERT   It is, isn't it? I never really look at it. I just—live
here.

APRIL   Oh, it's terribly clever. See how nicely all the
furniture is placed in areas to make it so warm and sweet
and tucked in.

ROBERT (*Amazed*)   How about that?

APRIL   And the choice of colors is so relaxing and simple
and masculine.

ROBERT (*Still surprised, nodding his head in agreement*)
See that!

APRIL   Isn't that tasteful and interesting?

ROBERT   Yes. I'll take it. (*They smile*) I mean I've always
liked my apartment, but I'm never really in it. I just seem
to pass through the living room on my way to the bedroom to get to the bathroom to get ready to go out again.

APRIL   You never really spend any time in here? And it's
so dear . . . But maybe that's why you like it so much.
If you don't spend much time in it, it keeps it special
and important.

ROBERT (*Amazed; slowly. He looks around*)   Yes. (*The
bed appears and moves downstage to its place opposite
them*) And this is the bedroom over here. (*She slowly
crosses to it apprehensively*) You love it, I can tell. Well,
I can always look for another place.

> (ROBERT *and* APRIL *begin to touch, embrace and
> then to kiss, all in very slow motion, as the lights
> come up on* SARAH *and* HARRY, *in their own apart-
> ment. They begin to sing "Poor Baby"*)

SARAH
   Darling—
HARRY
   Yes?
SARAH
   Robert—
HARRY
   What?
SARAH
   I worry—
HARRY
   Why?
SARAH
   He's all alone.
      (HARRY *grunts*)
   There's no one—
HARRY
   Where?
SARAH
   In his life.
HARRY
   Oh.
SARAH
   Robert ought to have a woman.
   Poor baby, all alone,
   Evening after evening by the telephone—
   We're the only tenderness he's ever known.
   Poor baby . . .
      (*The lights come up on* JENNY *and* DAVID, *in their
      apartment*)

JENNY
   David—
DAVID
   Yes?

88

JENNY
    Bobby—
DAVID
    What?
JENNY
    I worry.
DAVID
    Why?
JENNY
    It's such a waste.

        (DAVID *grunts*)

    There's no one.

DAVID
    Where?
JENNY
    In his life.
DAVID
    Oh.
JENNY
    Bobby ought to have a woman.
    Poor baby, sitting there,
    Staring at the walls and playing solitaire,
    Making conversation with the empty air—
    Poor baby.

    (*The lights go down on the couples*)

APRIL   Right after I became an airline stewardess, a friend
    of mine who had a garden apartment gave me a cocoon
    for my bedroom. He collects things like that, insects and
    caterpillars and all that . . . It was attached to a twig, and
    he said one morning I'd wake up to a beautiful butterfly
    in *my* bedroom—when it hatched. He told me that when
    they come out they're soaking wet, and there is a drop
    of blood there too—isn't that fascinating?—but within

an hour they dry off and then they begin to fly. Well, I told him I had a cat. I had a cat then, but he said just put the cocoon somewhere where the cat couldn't get at it—which is impossible, but what can you do? So I put it up high on a ledge where the cat never went, and the next morning it was still there, at least, so it seemed safe to leave it. Well, anyway, almost a week later very, very early this one morning the guy calls me, and he said, "April, do you have a butterfly this morning?" I told him to hold on, and managed to get up and look, and there on that ledge I saw this wet spot and a little speck of blood but no butterfly, and I thought "Oh, dear God in Heaven, the cat got it." I picked up the phone to tell this guy and just then suddenly I spotted it under the dressing table—it was moving one wing. The cat had got at it, but it was still alive. So I told the guy, and he got so upset, and he said "Oh no! Oh, God, no! Don't you see that's a life—a living thing?" Well, I got dressed and took it to the park and put it on a rose—it was summer then—and it looked like it was going to be all right—I think, anyway. But that man . . . I really felt damaged by him—awful—that was just cruel. I got home and I called him back and said, "Listen, I'm a living thing too, you shithead!" (*A pause*) I never saw him again.

ROBERT (*He stands staring—too stunned to move. They are both standing in the bedroom doorway. There is a pause*) That reminds me of something I did to someone once . . . in Miami. I mean . . . it's not really the same, but in a way. Well, you'll see. I met a girl, a lovely girl, at a party one night and, well, it was like you and me, April. We just—connected. You don't mind my telling this, do you?

APRIL   No.

ROBERT It just . . . came to my mind. Anyway, we just connected, in such a beautiful way . . . exactly like to-night. Except we couldn't even contain ourselves. It was incredible. We were talking and suddenly we realized we just couldn't talk any more. No sounds came. We stood looking at each other and we were both bathed in per-spiration. Our breathing was so short and our legs were trembling and we just left. We drove to one of those strips there where they have all those motels, and we didn't even say anything. She just sat so close to me. So close. We got inside that room and we started touching and kissing and laughing and holding, and suddenly she said I should go get lots of champagne and some baby oil and we should get beautifully high and then rub . . . well, you know. She said she'd be in bed waiting for me. (APRIL *is visibly turned on by this story*) I rushed out of there and I drove around until I could find a liquor store and a drugstore open, and I got all this champagne and the oil and finally I started back to the motel and—I —could not—find—it. (APRIL *almost faints*) I looked for over three hours. I never found it. And I never saw her again either.

APRIL (*Her breathing is heavy and raspy—she has identified totally with "the girl"*) Oh. That is the most extraordi-nary story I have ever heard. (ROBERT *slowly helps her out of her jacket and starts unzipping her blouse. She is almost mesmerized*) That poor girl. (ROBERT *kneels and takes off one of her shoes; she immediately offers her foot*) And you drove around for three hours?

ROBERT More!

(*Now they both start undressing rapidly, dropping or tossing their clothes anywhere. He pulls back the bedspread on both sides.* APRIL *sits on it and unrolls her stockings)*

ROBERT   All night I tried to find that motel. All night. With the oil and all that champagne and my hands trembling and sweat running down my face.

(She has begun to cry a little bit for "the girl"—she is under the covers now, doing the last of her undressing under the covers)

APRIL   Oh, that girl. She never knew. Oh. Well, I just don't know what to say or do. That's so sad!

ROBERT   I know. It is. Very.

APRIL   But, Robert, those stories don't really follow. I don't see the connection. (ROBERT *gives an "Oh, my God, caught" look)* Unless . . . oh . . . you must have thought of that poor girl as the wounded butterfly . . .

ROBERT *(Takes out champagne, glasses and baby oil)*   Yes, that's it!

(The lights go down on the bedroom and come up on SARAH *and* JENNY, *together. They sing)*

SARAH
   Robert.
JENNY
   Bobby.
SARAH
   Robert angel . . .
JENNY
   Bobby honey . . .

SARAH

> You know, no one
> Wants you to be happy
> More than I do.
> No one, but
> Isn't she a little bit, well,
> You know,
> Face it. Why her?
> Better, no one . . .

JENNY

> . . . wants you to be happy
> More than I do.
> No one, but . . .

SARAH and JENNY

> . . . isn't she a little bit,
> Well, you know, face it.
> (SUSAN *joins them*)

SUSAN

> You know, no one
> Wants you to be happy
> More than I do.
> (AMY *and* JOANNE *join them*)

AMY and JOANNE

> You know, no one
> Wants you to be happy
> More than I do. No one, but . . .

ALL

> Isn't she a little bit, well . . .

SARAH

> Dumb? Where is she from?

AMY

> Tacky? Neurotic? She seems so dead.

SUSAN

> Vulgar? Aggressive? Peculiar?

JENNY

    Old? And cheap and

JOANNE

    Tall? She's tall enough to be your mother.

SARAH

    She's very weird . . .

JENNY

    Gross and . . .

SUSAN

    Depressing, and . . .

AMY

    And immature . . .

JOANNE

    Goliath,

ALL

    Poor baby,
    All alone,
    Throw a lonely dog a bone,
    It's still a bone.
    We're the only tenderness
    He's ever known.
    Poor baby.

> *(The lights go down on the women and the bedroom disappears. Now* KATHY *appears and begins to dance. Throughout the number* ROBERT *and* APRIL's *voices are heard.* KATHY's *dance expresses the difference between having sex and making love. During the dialogue between* ROBERT *and* APRIL, *she dances the "having sex"; during the rest of the sequence, the "making love")*

ROBERT   Oh, this is sensational . . .

APRIL   Oh, I think he really likes me.

94

(KATHY *changes her dance step and/or movement*)

ROBERT   Wow, she's nice.

APRIL   He's so nice.

ROBERT   Oh, God.

APRIL   Oh, dear.

ROBERT   Oh.

APRIL   Oh.

ROBERT   I like that.

APRIL   I love that.

(KATHY *changes her dance step and/or movement*)

ROBERT   Oh, she has such a smooth body.

APRIL   What is he doing?

(KATHY *changes her dance step and/or movement*)

ROBERT   With all that long hair I can't even find her head.

APRIL   He really likes me. (KATHY *changes her dance step and/or movement*) It's poetry.

ROBERT   It's beautiful.

APRIL   I think I could love him.

ROBERT   If only I could remember her name.

(KATHY *changes her dance step and/or movement*)

APRIL   He smells so good.

ROBERT   She tastes so good.

APRIL   He feels so good.

ROBERT   What is her name?

> (KATHY *changes her dance step and/or movement.
> We hear the voices of the married couples*)

APRIL   I love you, I love you . . .

ROBERT   I . . . I . . .

> (KATHY *changes her dance step and/or movement*)

SARAH   I love you, Harry.

HARRY   I love you, Sarah.

JENNY   I love you, David.

DAVID   I love you, Jenny.

ALL   I love you, I love you, I love you . . .

> (*After the dance, the lights come up on the bed-
> room as before.* ROBERT *has his hand over his eyes;
> both he and* APRIL *are completely exhausted. The
> alarm clock goes off.* APRIL *shuts off the clock and
> turns on a light. She begins gathering her clothes.
> They sing*)

ROBERT
   Where you going?

APRIL

Barcelona.

ROBERT

. . . oh . . .

APRIL

Don't get up.

ROBERT

Do you have to?

APRIL

Yes, I have to.

ROBERT

. . . oh . . .

APRIL

Don't get up.
(*Pauses*)
Now you're angry.

ROBERT

No, I'm not.

APRIL

Yes, you are.

ROBERT

No, I'm not.
Put your things down.

APRIL

See, you're angry.

ROBERT

No, I'm not.

APRIL

Yes, you are.

ROBERT

No, I'm not.
Put your wings down
And stay.

APRIL

    I'm leaving.

ROBERT

    Why?

APRIL

    To go to—

ROBERT

    Stay—

APRIL

    I have to—

APRIL and ROBERT

    Fly—

ROBERT

    I know—

APRIL and ROBERT

    To Barcelona.

ROBERT

    Look,
    You're a very special girl,
    Not just overnight.
    No, you're a very special girl,
    And not because you're bright—
    Not *just* because you're bright.

      (*Yawning*)

    You're just a very special girl,
    June!

APRIL

    April . . .

ROBERT

    April . . .

      (*There is a pause*)

APRIL

    Thank you.

ROBERT
Whatcha thinking?

APRIL
Barcelona.

ROBERT
. . . oh . . .

APRIL
Flight Eighteen.

ROBERT
Stay a minute.

APRIL
I would like to.

ROBERT
. . . so? . . .

APRIL
Don't be mean.

ROBERT
Stay a minute.

APRIL
No, I can't.

ROBERT
Yes, you can.

APRIL
No, I can't.

ROBERT
Where you going?

APRIL
Barcelona.

ROBERT
So you said—

APRIL
And Madrid.

ROBERT
Bon voyage.

APRIL
> On a Boeing.

ROBERT
> Good night.

APRIL
> You're angry.

ROBERT
> No.

APRIL
> I've got to—

ROBERT
> Right.

APRIL
> Report to—

ROBERT
> Go.

APRIL
> That's not to
> Say
> That if I had my way . . .
> Oh well, I guess okay.

ROBERT
> What?

APRIL
> I'll stay.

ROBERT
> But . . .
> *(As she snuggles down)*
> Oh, God!

Blackout

SCENE THREE

The scene is PETER *and* SUSAN's *terrace.* ROBERT *and* MARTA *come up in the elevator.* PETER *and* SUSAN *are basking in the sun on the terrace.*

SUSAN Oh, Peter, look who's here. It's Robert. And you must be Marta.

MARTA (*Leans over the railing*) Oh, God, look! You can see the East River.

ROBERT I'm surprised to find you out on the terrace. It's terrific.

SUSAN Peter fixed it all up. Oh, Marta, I'm so glad Robert brought you by. You are just what he said . . . so pretty and original and pecul—I mean . . .

MARTA Right!

SUSAN Well, now, Robert, how have *you* been?

ROBERT You know me. I'm always happy. (*All heads turn and stare at him, astonished. He is taken aback*) What did I say?

PETER (*After an awkward moment*) Hey, Bob, did Susan show you the pictures I took in Mexico when I went down to get the divorce?

ROBERT   Divorce? You're not married now?

SUSAN   Not since the divorce.

ROBERT   Oh.

PETER   I flew down to Mexico. It is absolutely sensational down there. It is so terrific, I phoned Susan to come down and join me.

SUSAN   It's so pretty down there.

ROBERT   Where are you living now, Peter?

PETER   Well, here at home. I mean I've got responsibilities . . . Susan and the kids to take care of. I certainly wouldn't leave them.

ROBERT   It sure seems to be working.

SUSAN   Well, my goodness! We're all four single. It's nicer, I think. Especially if you have somebody.

(SUSAN *and* PETER *embrace*)

MARTA   Now *this* is what I call New York!

Blackout

SCENE FOUR

The stage is alive with the activity of a private night-club. There are running waiters and, in a cage to one side, a go-go girl.

JOANNE *and* ROBERT *are seated at a table on stage level, watching* JOANNE's *husband,* LARRY, *dance with one of the patrons.* JOANNE *and* ROBERT *grow increasingly drunk as the scene progresses. She is an acerbic drunk.* ROBERT *laughs and gets silly, but never really loses himself.* LARRY *is quite decent and quite sober, but having a wonderful time)*

ROBERT   I think they're going to hurt themselves.

JOANNE   What if their mothers came in and saw them up there doing that? Think of their poor mothers. He's embarrassing.

ROBERT   Anyway, those people that laugh and carry on and dance like that—they're not happy.

JOANNE (*She yells in* LARRY's *direction*)   Think of your poor mother!

ROBERT   He's not what you'd call self-conscious.

JOANNE   He's not what you'd call! Big show-off. It really shocks me to see a grown man dance like that! (*Yelling to* LARRY *again*) I am shocked, you hear, shocked! (*To* ROBERT) Where was I? Oh—my first husband. He is so difficult to remember. Even when you're with him. We got married here in New York. See, he was here on some business deal, but he owned a big meat-packing company in Chicago. Attractive? Well, we lived in New York for almost a year and then one day he had to go back to Chicago. And, you know, he was actually surprised when I told him I would just wait here for him. I mean, I still really don't know quite where Chicago is. It's over there somewhere. (*She points vaguely*) He said he didn't really plan to come back . . . So I knew we were in a tiny dilemma—or at least he was. I was still too young. But I was old enough to know where I was living, and I had no intention of leaving New York. I have never left New York. Never have, never will. And least of all would I ever want to go to a place where they actually feel honored being called "hog butcher for the world." I said, "Kiss off, Rodney," but I said it nicer. Well, we got a divorce. A divorce. Huh! One word means all of that. Another drink, guy . . . sir. *Oh, sir!*

> (*The waiters are too busy and ignore her. The dance ends; everyone applauds.* LARRY *and his partner say goodbye, and he crosses to* JOANNE's *table and stands there catching his breath.* LARRY *has a red flower in his lapel*)

LARRY   Whew!

JOANNE (*Looking up at him and away*)   We already gave.

LARRY (*Sits; looks at* ROBERT)   You all had a few while I was dancing, huh?

JOANNE   Larry, what the hell was all that carrying on? What was that? Shocking. (*Yells to passing waiters*) SIR! SIR! *TROIS ENCORE, S'IL VOUS PLAÎT!*

LARRY (*Looks at* JOANNE) I asked you to dance.

JOANNE I only dance when you can touch. I don't think standing bumping around and making an ass out of oneself is a dance. I find it unbelievably humiliating watching my own husband flouncing around the dance floor, jerking and sashaying all over the place like Ann Miller. Take off the red shoes, Larry. Off.

LARRY (*To* ROBERT) Was I that good?

ROBERT Very. Excellent. Amazingly good.

LARRY (*Laughing*) Joanne, I love you when you're jealous. Kiss me.

JOANNE I hated dinner. I hated the opera, and I hate it here. What I need is more to drink—and look at Bobby, how desperately he needs another drink. (*The waiters enter again. The female patrons are seen seated at various tables*) Here they come again. SIR! DRINKS HERE—TWO MORE BOURBONS AND A VODKA STINGER! Do you know that we are suddenly at an age where we find ourselves too young for the old people and too old for the young ones? We're nowhere. I think we better drink to us. To us—the generation gap. WE ARE THE GENERATION GAP! (*The other women in the club turn and stare at her*) Are they staring at me? Let 'em stare—let 'em, those broads. What else have they got to do—all dressed up with no place to go.

LARRY What time is it?

JOANNE In real life? Will somebody get us another drink! (*At this point each of the four waiters delivers a round of drinks to the table)* Oh, you did. So aggressive. *(To the other women)* STOP STARING! *(There is a blackout on the night-club, leaving her alone in a spotlight; she turns to the audience)* I'd like to propose a toast. *(She sings)*

Here's to the ladies who lunch—
Everybody laugh.
Lounging in their caftans and planning a brunch
On their own behalf.
Off to the gym,
Then to a fitting,
Claiming they're fat.
And looking grim
'Cause they've been sitting
Choosing a hat—
    (She stands)
Does anyone still wear a hat?
I'll drink to that.

Here's to the girls who stay smart—
Aren't they a gas?
Rushing to their classes in optical art,
Wishing it would pass.
Another long exhausting day,
Another thousand dollars,
A matinée, a Pinter play,
Perhaps a piece of Mahler's—
I'll drink to that.
And one for Mahler.

Here's to the girls who play wife—
Aren't they too much?
Keeping house but clutching a copy of *Life*
Just to keep in touch.
The ones who follow the rules,

And meet themselves at the schools,
Too busy to know that they're fools—
Aren't they a gem?
I'll drink to them.
Let's all drink to them.

And here's to the girls who just watch—
Aren't they the best?
When they get depressed, it's a bottle of Scotch
Plus a little jest.
Another chance to disapprove,
Another brilliant zinger,
Another reason not to move,
Another vodka stinger—
Aaaahh—I'll drink to that.

So here's to the girls on the go—
Everybody tries.
Look into their eyes and you'll see what they know:
Everybody dies.
A toast to that invincible bunch—
The dinosaurs surviving the crunch—
Let's hear it for the ladies who lunch—
Everybody rise! Rise!
Rise! Rise! Rise! Rise! Rise! Rise!

(*She sits as the lights come up on the night-club again*)

I would like a cigarette, Larry. (*He gives her one and lights it*) Remember when everyone used to smoke? How it was more—uh—festive, happier or something. Now every place is not unlike an operating room, for Chrissake.

(*Pokes* ROBERT)

Huh?

ROBERT   I never smoked.

JOANNE   Why?

ROBERT   I don't know. I meant to. Does that count?

JOANNE   Meant to! Meant to! Story of your life. Meant to! Jesus, you are lifted right out of a Krafft-Ebing case history. You were always outside looking in the window while everybody was inside dancing at the party. Now I insist you smoke. Your first compromise. (*Shouts at the waiters again*) OH, SIR, MORE CIGARETTES PLEASE! THESE ARE FINE. LETHAL. (*She tears the package open completely*) Here, Rob! Smoke!

ROBERT   No, thank you.

LARRY   Joanne, honey, c'mon—he doesn't.

ROBERT   You smoke. I'll watch.

JOANNE   Watch? Did you hear yourself? Huh? Hear what you just said, kiddo? Watch. I am offering you . . .

ROBERT (*Interrupting*)   I don't want one.

JOANNE (*Angry*)   Because you're weak . . . (*Throws the pack down*) I hate people who are weak! (*Takes a deep drag and exhales*) That's the best. Better than Librium. Smoking may be the only thing that separates us from the lower forms.

LARRY   You wanna split?

JOANNE   Of what?

LARRY We don't act like this when you're not here, Robby. I wish you could meet Joanne sometime. She's really great. In fact, when you marry, be sure you marry a girl just like her . . .

JOANNE (*Sarcastically, really putting* ROBERT *down*) Don't ever get married, Robby. Never. Why should you?

ROBERT For company, I don't know. Like everybody else.

JOANNE Who else?

ROBERT Everybody that ever fell in love and got married.

JOANNE I know both couples and they're both divorced. Oh, Larry, you interrupted me before. See what happens when you rush me. I wanted to toast my second husband.

LARRY (*Getting up*) I'm going to the john. And when I come back, we'll be leaving shortly. The holiday is ending. Okay?

(*He goes out*)

ROBERT (*Calling after* LARRY) I got the check. Damn. I know he's off to pay the check. (JOANNE *sits with a drink in one hand and a cigarette in the other and doesn't take her eyes off* ROBERT) Or maybe buy the place. It is a comfort to have rich friends. But I do like to pay some of the time. Oh, well, you talked me into it! (*Pauses. He becomes increasingly uncomfortable*) You have a good third husband, Joanne. He's a good man. Anyway, thank you for the evening. I'm glad I joined you. I was really feeling low . . . really depressed. I drank, but you really put it away tonight. The last several times you and I got together, I've had shameful hangovers—abominable.

We may be doing permanent damage—think of that! I
don't know what to think of the fact that you only drink
with me . . . I guess, that is not unflattering. No! I hope
I don't depress you! We have good times and it's a hoot,
yes? Whatever you say! (*Pauses*) No. I don't care for a
cigarette if that is what you're trying to stare me into.
Even though I am a product of my generation, I still do
not smoke. My age group is a very uptight age group.
Middle age is breaking up that old gang of mine. Whew!
It's very drunk out tonight. What are you looking at,
Joanne? It's my charisma, huh? Well, stop looking at
my charisma!

JOANNE (*Still staring; no change in position or voice*)
When are we gonna make it?

ROBERT (*A pause*) I beg your pardon?

JOANNE When're we gonna make it?

ROBERT (*Making light of it*) What's wrong with now?

JOANNE (*Slowly, directly, sultrily, quietly and evenly*)
There's my place. It's free tomorrow at two. Larry goes
to his gym then. Don't talk. Don't do your folksy Harold
Teen with me. You're a terribly attractive man. The
kind of a man most women want and never seem to get.
I'll—take care of you.

ROBERT (*A pause. He's been looking down; he looks up*)
But who will I take care of?

JOANNE (*A big smile*) Well, did you hear yourself? Did
you hear what you just said, kiddo?

(*The discotheque music begins again*)

LARRY (*Reenters*) Well, the check is paid and . . . (*Looks at a stunned* ROBERT) What's wrong?

ROBERT I didn't mean that.

LARRY What's wrong?

ROBERT (*Getting angry*) I've looked at all that—marriages and all that—and what do you get for it? What do you get?

> (ROBERT *leaves the table. The music of "Bobby Baby" is heard in the orchestra*)

LARRY What happened?

JOANNE I just did someone a big favor. C'mon, Larry, let's go home.

> (*The music of "Bobby Baby" is heard in the orchestra.* JOANNE *and* LARRY *leave the night-club table and return to their living area above. The husbands enter and join their wives—who were already seated in the living areas as the female patrons in the night-club scene. The stage is cleared.* ROBERT *is center stage*)

ROBERT What do you get?

JENNY (*Sings*)
    Bobby . . .
PETER
    Bobby . . .
AMY
    Bobby baby . . .
PAUL
    Bobby bubi . . .

HARRY
    Robby . . .
SARAH
    Robert darling . . .

DAVID
    Bobby, we've been trying to call you.
JENNY
    Bobby . . .
LARRY
    Bobby . . .
AMY
    Bobby baby . . .
PAUL
    Bobby bubi . . .

SARAH
    Angel, I've got something to tell you.
HARRY
    Bob . . .
LARRY
    Rob-o . . .
JOANNE
    Bobby love . . .
SUSAN
    Bobby honey . . .

AMY and PAUL
    Bobby, we've been trying to reach you all day.
LARRY
    Bobby . . .
HARRY
    Bobby . . .
PETER
    Bobby baby . . .

SARAH
   Angel . . .
JOANNE
   Darling . . .

DAVID and JENNY
   The kids were asking, Bobby . . .
HARRY
   Bobby . . .
SUSAN
   Robert . . .
JOANNE
   Robby . . .
PETER
   Bob-o . . .

LARRY and JOANNE
   Bobby, there was something we wanted to say.
SARAH and HARRY
   Bobby . . .
PAUL
   Bobby bubi . . .
AMY
   Sweetheart . . .
SUSAN
   Sugar . . .

DAVID and JENNY
   Your line was busy.
ALL
   Bobby . . .

ROBERT (*Shouts; angry*)   Stop! What do you get?
   (*He sings "Being Alive"*)
   Someone to hold you too close,

> Someone to hurt you too deep,
> Someone to sit in your chair,
> To ruin your sleep . . .

PAUL That's true, but there's more than that.

SARAH Is that all you think there is to it?

HARRY You've got so many reasons for not being with someone, but Robert, you haven't got one good reason for being alone.

LARRY Come on. You're on to something, Bobby. You're on to something.

ROBERT
> Someone to need you too much,
> Someone to know you too well,
> Someone to pull you up short
> And put you through hell . . .

DAVID You see what you look for, you know.

JOANNE You're not a kid any more, Robby, and I don't think you'll ever be a kid again, kiddo.

PETER Hey, buddy, don't be afraid it won't be perfect . . . The only thing to be afraid of really is that it won't *be*!

JENNY Don't stop now! Keep going!

ROBERT
> Someone you have to let in,
> Someone whose feelings you spare,
> Someone who, like it or not, will want you to share
> A little, a lot . . .

SUSAN   And what does all that mean?

LARRY   Robert, how do you know so much about it when you've never been there?

HARRY   It's all much better living it than looking at it, Robert.

PETER   Add 'em up, Bobby, add 'em up.

ROBERT
Someone to crowd you with love,
Someone to force you to care,
Someone to make you come through,
Who'll always be there, as frightened as you,
Of being alive,
Being alive, being alive, being alive.

AMY   Blow out the candles, Robert, and make a wish.
Want something! Want *something!*
(*Robert, touched and hurting, closes his eyes and clenches his fists*)

ROBERT
Somebody hold me too close,
Somebody hurt me too deep,
Somebody sit in my chair
And ruin my sleep and make me aware
Of being alive, being alive.

(*The lights go down on the couples, leaving* ROBERT *alone on stage* ROBERT *opens his eyes*)
Somebody need me too much,
Somebody know me too well,
Somebody pull me up short

And put me through hell and give me support
For being alive.
Make me alive.
Make me confused, mock me with praise,
Let me be used, vary my days.
But alone is alone, not alive.

Somebody crowd me with love,
Somebody force me to care,
Somebody let me come through.
I'll always be there, as frightened as you,
To help us survive
Being alive, being alive, being alive.

(*The lights come up on the birthday party in* ROBERT's *apartment again*)

The scene is Robert's apartment. There is an atmosphere of apprehension this time.
We hear footsteps in the distance, growing louder. The lights are turned down, a key is heard in a lock—but it is another door that opens and closes. There are a few seconds of silence.

LARRY (*More seriously than we're used to*) Must have been the apartment across the hall.

HARRY (*A pause*) This is the craziest thing . . . huh?

AMY Do you think something's wrong?

PAUL No.

AMY Neither do I.

PETER I do. I've called every joint in town.

SUSAN It *has* been over two hours now. Maybe he forgot.

SARAH How can anyone forget a surprise birthday?

JOANNE Or . . . maybe the surprise is on us. I think I got the message. C'mon, Larry, let's go home.

LARRY Yeah. I think we should.

AMY (*A pause*) Let's go, Paul.

PAUL Yes, I think we can now.

SARAH (*Quietly*) Maybe we should leave him a note.

HARRY (*Gently, to* SARAH) Maybe we ought to leave him be.

SUSAN I'll call him tomorrow.

PETER (*In deep thought*) Don't.

SUSAN (*Very quietly*) I won't.

JENNY David?

DAVID What?

JENNY Nothing.

JOANNE (*Gathering all around the table*) Okay. All together, everybody.

ALL Happy birthday, Robert!

> (*They blow out the candles and the lights go out in the apartment. Throughout this scene,* ROBERT *has stood center stage, listening; now he smiles*)

> *Curtain*

About the Authors

GEORGE FURTH was born in 1932 in Chicago. After his graduation from Northwestern University, he went East to get a master's degree from Columbia University. Then he entered the theater as an actor, becoming a member of the Actors Studio. His first Broadway performance (in *A Cook for Mr. General,* 1961) brought him a contract at Universal Studios, where he remained doing television and motion picture work for five years. He has appeared in fifteen movies, including *Butch Cassidy and the Sundance Kid, Myra Breckinridge, The Boston Strangler, What's So Bad About Feeling Good* and *The Best Man.* A most prolific actor, George Furth has appeared on virtually every major television show, and has been a regular on four series.

The book for *Company* is Mr. Furth's first attempt at writing. *Company* has received the New York Drama Critics' Circle and Outer Circle awards for the best musical of the 1969–1970 season, and a Best Play citation. Mr. Furth's next play is a nonmusical entitled *A Chorus Line.*

STEPHEN SONDHEIM is the creator of the memorable lyrics for *West Side Story.* Born in 1930 in New York City, he attended Williams College, where he won the Hutchinson Prize for Musical Composition. After graduating, he studied theory and composition with Milton Babbitt. Mr. Sondheim composed the incidental music for Broadway's *Girls of Summer* and *Invitation to a March.* He wrote the lyrics for *Gypsy* and *Do I Hear a Waltz?* and was responsible for both the lyrics and music of *A Funny Thing Happened on the Way to the Forum* and *Anyone Can Whistle* and, now, *Company.* In addition, he has written scripts for the television series *Topper,* and was until recently the author of brain-teasing crossword puzzles in *New York Magazine.* Mr. Sondheim is currently completing *Follies,* a show for production in the 1970–1971 season, with a libretto by James Goldman.